S0-ALA-096

Low Fat
Recipe
Secrets

The Low Fat Version of Your Favorite Foods

Ron Douglas

LOW FAT RECIPE SECRETS
The Low Fat Version of Your Favorite Foods

By Ron Douglas

Copyright © 2007, SendMeRecipes.com
All rights reserved

This book, nor any portion thereof, may not be stored in a retrieval system, transmitted, scanned, or otherwise copied or reproduced by any means in any form without prior written permission of both the author and copyright owner.

Printed in the United States of America

Published and distributed by Verity Associates, LLC - Kew Gardens Hills NY

LIMITS OF LIABILITY AND WARRANTY DISCLAIMER. Author and publisher make no warranty of any kind, expressed or implied, regarding the information contained in this book, and shall not be liable in any event for incidental or consequential damages in connection with, or arising out of, the furnishing or usage of information contained herein. This book is for information purposes only and should not be construed to be medical, nutritional, or professional advice.

Preface

These days everyone seems to be trying to lose weight and eat healthier. Just look at all of the fad diets and flavor or the month exercise programs out there selling dreams of physical fitness.

Many people work really hard following these programs only to put the weight back on within 6 months. That's because they're not addressing the real issue. The real issue is, we all love to eat good food. It's one of the joys of life. The problem is, the food you love the most is usually the worst for you.

Eating healthy and keeping the weight off is not a sprint, it's a marathon. It's a change of lifestyle. It calls for a long term change in your eating habits. Yes, I know, it's easier said than done.

Wouldn't it be nice if there was a way you could keep the weight off while still eating food that you love? Wouldn't it be great to have a collection of recipes at your side which taste great but are actually less fattening? That was our mission in creating this cookbook - to make losing weight easier by providing you incredibly delicious low fat dishes!

This cookbook is a compilation of recipes originally published on our website SendMeRecipes.com (SMR). SMR is a meal planning service which many have successfully used to lose weight, save time in the kitchen, and live a healthier lifestyle.

You can read some of the SMR success stories and get a Free Trial Membership - go to: **www.SendMeRecipes.com**

Table of Contents

Entrees   37

Appetizers

Asian Meatballs
Balsamic and Tomato Bruschetta
Cauliflower Poppers
Cumin Pita Wedges With Spicy Hummus
Herb Curry Dip
Hoppin' Jalapenos!
Nachos
Oriental Mushroom Appetizer
Rice-Stuffed Grape Leaves
Roasted Eggplant Basil Spread
Roasted Eggplant Crostini
Shrimp Marinated In Lime and Dijon Mustard
Southwestern Potato Skins
Stuffed Cucumber Appetizers
Tri-Color Mediterranean Salsa

Asian Meatballs

10 oz ground skinless turkey breast
1/2 green bell pepper, seeded and minced
4 scallions, thinly sliced
1/3 cup fine dried bread crumbs
2 Tbs minced water chestnuts
1 egg white
1 Tbs reduced-sodium soy sauce
1/4 cup sweet and sour sauce
1/2 cup unsweetened apple sauce

Preheat the oven to 375 degrees. Spray a nonstick jelly-roll pan with nonstick cooking spray.

In a medium bowl, lightly combine the turkey, pepper, scallions, bread crumbs, water chestnuts, egg white and soy sauce. Shape into 32 equal meatballs, about 1" each; place on the pan. Bake until cooked through and browned, about 15 minutes.

Meanwhile, in a 2-quart microwavable dish, combine the sweet and sour sauce and applesauce; microwave on High until hot and bubbling, 2 minutes. Stir in the meatballs and serve with toothpicks.

Serves 8

Nutrition Facts

Nutrition (per serving): 82.0 calories; 9% calories from fat; 1.0g total fat; 22.0mg cholesterol; 163.0mg sodium; 9.0g carbohydrates; 1.0g fiber; 12.0g protein.

Balsamic and Tomato Bruschetta

1 pint cherry tomatoes, chopped
1/4 cup fresh basil, chopped
2 Tbs extra-virgin olive oil
1 Tbs balsamic vinegar
1 garlic clove, minced
1/2 tsp salt
Freshly-ground black pepper, to taste
1/2 tsp sugar
1 baguette - (abt 20
1 garlic clove
2 Tbs grated Parmesan cheese

Combine the chopped tomatoes, basil, olive oil, vinegar, minced garlic, salt, pepper and sugar in a bowl. Toss.

Cut the baguette into 4 pieces. Slice in half lengthwise and place on baking sheet. Toast in a 400 degree oven for about 10 minutes; turn once. Remove when crusty on both sides.

Rub bread with the garlic clove. Spoon the tomato mixture over the bread and sprinkle with Parmesan cheese. Serve immediately.

Serves 8

Nutrition Facts

Nutrition (per serving): 150.0 calories; 30% calories from fat; 5.0g total fat; 1.0mg cholesterol; 450.0mg sodium; 21.0g carbohydrates; 1.0g fiber; 5.0g protein.

Cauliflower Poppers

1 small cauliflower head
1/2 tsp ground cumin
1/2 tsp chili powder, or more to taste
1/2 tsp table salt
1/2 tsp freshly-ground black pepper
1 serving cooking spray

Preheat oven to 400 degrees. Cut cauliflower florets into grape-sized pieces. (There should be about 4 cups.) Place cauliflower in a medium bowl; add cumin, chili powder, salt and pepper and toss well to coat.

Coat baking sheet with cooking spray. Spread cauliflower on sheet and bake until cauliflower is tender, but not mushy, stirring halfway through, about 10 minutes.

Comments: The spicy taste of these tempting morsels can be addictive. Not to worry, though. They are light enough to be eaten with abandon.

Serves 8

Nutrition Facts

Nutrition (per serving): 2.5 calories; 50% calories from fat; 0.1g total fat; 0.0mg cholesterol; 147.7mg sodium; 12.1mg potassium; 0.3g carbohydrates; 0.1g fiber; 0.1g sugar; 0.1g protein.

Cumin Pita Wedges With Spicy Hummus

6 small wheat pitas, cut 6 wedges each
6 servings olive oil cooking spray = (or enough to coat pitas)
2 tsp ground cumin
1/2 tsp table salt
15 1/2 oz canned chickpeas, rinsed, drained
15 1/2 oz canned small white beans, rinsed, drained
3 Tbs tahini
2 Tbs fresh lemon juice
2 medium garlic cloves, chopped
1 tsp hot picante sauce, or to taste = (or other hot sauce)

Preheat oven to 400 degrees. Coat a large baking sheet with cooking spray.

Place pita wedges on baking sheet and lightly coat with cooking spray; sprinkle with cumin and salt. Bake until golden brown, about 8 to 10 minutes.

Meanwhile, to make hummus, combine remaining ingredients in a food processor and process until smooth. If you don't have a food processor, use a blender or mash the ingredients together with a fork.

Serve hummus with pita wedges on the side.

Serves 12

Nutrition Facts

Nutrition (per serving): 237.1 calories; 19% calories from fat; 5.4g total fat; 0.0mg cholesterol; 300.8mg sodium; 704.6mg potassium; 37.5g carbohydrates; 7.9g fiber; 1.0g sugar; 11.7g protein.

Herb Curry Dip

1 cup fat-free mayonnaise
1/2 cup fat-free sour cream
1 tsp crushed fine herbs
1/8 tsp curry powder
1 Tbs chopped fresh parsley
1 Tbs grated onion
1 1/2 tsp lemon juice
1/2 tsp Worcestershire sauce
2 tsp capers, (optional)

Combine all ingredients. Mix well. Refrigerate. Great to dip grapes, pineapple or celery into.

This recipe yields six 1/4-cup servings.

Serves 6

Nutrition Facts

Nutrition (per serving): 47.0 calories; 360.0mg sodium; 10.0g carbohydrates; 1.0g protein.

Hoppin' Jalapenos!

12 fresh whole jalapeño peppers
3 oz low-fat cream cheese, room temperature
1/2 cup fine-shredded low-fat sharp Cheddar cheese
1/4 cup finely-chopped green onions

Carefully cut each jalapeño lengthwise. Under running water, rinse out the seeds and remove the stems and veins. In a small mixing bowl, mix cheeses and onions. Use a small spoon to stuff each jalapeño half with the cheese mixture.

Bake the peppers in a 350 degree oven for about 15 minutes, or until the cheese melts.

Serves 12

Nutrition Facts

Nutrition (per serving): 55.0 calories; 32% calories from fat; 2.0g total fat; 5.0mg cholesterol; 63.0mg sodium; 1.0g fiber.

Nachos

8 corn tortillas
2 medium tomatoes, chopped - (2 cups)
4 green onions including green tops, thinly sliced
1 garlic clove
2 Tbs chopped fresh cilantro or parsley
1 Tbs red-wine vinegar
1/4 cup shredded reduced-fat Monterey Jack cheese
1/4 cup shredded reduced-fat cheddar cheese

Preheat oven to 350 degrees. Cut tortillas into quarters. Place in single layer onto baking sheet. Bake until crisp -- about 5 minutes. (Watch closely -- don't let burn.) Remove from oven. Turn temperature to broil.

Combine chopped tomatoes, onions, garlic, cilantro or parsley, and vinegar in a bowl. Mix well. Place about 2 teaspoons of salsa onto each chip. Top each with shredded cheeses. Return to oven and broil about 4 inches from heat until cheese melts. Place nachos onto platter. Serve immediately.

Serves 4

Nutrition Facts

Nutrition (per serving): 215.0 calories; 25% calories from fat; 6.0g total fat; 13.0mg cholesterol; 180.0mg sodium; 30.0g carbohydrates; 4.0g fiber; 10.0g protein.

Oriental Mushroom Appetizer

1 lb small to medium white mushrooms
1/4 cup water
2 Tbs white vinegar
2 Tbs soy sauce
4 garlic cloves, peeled, chopped
Freshly-ground black pepper, to taste
Splash of sesame oil
4 Tbs chopped parsley

Put mushrooms, water, vinegar, soy sauce and garlic into a saucepan with a tight-fitting lid; cover and bring to a boil. Reduce heat and simmer about 15 minutes. Uncover and simmer until the liquid is reduced by half. Add pepper and a splash of sesame oil. Toss with parsley. Serve with toothpicks.

Serves 6

Nutrition Facts

Nutrition (per serving): 24.4 calories; 9% calories from fat; 0.3g total fat; 0.0mg cholesterol; 205.0mg sodium; 275.4mg potassium; 4.1g carbohydrates; 1.1g fiber; 1.5g sugar; 2.9g protein.

Rice-Stuffed Grape Leaves

1 cup uncooked brown rice, (not instant)
1 cup chopped yellow onion
1/4 cup dill, fresh, chopped
1/4 cup mint leaves, fresh, chopped
4 cups reduced-sodium fat-free chicken broth
= (or vegetable broth)
1/4 cup fresh lemon juice
4 1/2 oz grape leaves - (abt 32 leaves), rinsed if canned

Combine rice, onion, dill and mint in a large nonstick skillet and set pan over medium heat. Sauté until onion is soft, stirring frequently to prevent rice from burning, about 5 minutes. Add 2 cups of broth, reduce heat to low, cover and simmer until rice is tender, about 25 minutes. Stir in lemon juice and remove from heat.

Place grape leaves, shiny-side down, on a flat surface. Top each leaf with 1 heaping teaspoon of rice mixture, placing filling near stem end of leaf. Fold in sides of leaf and then roll up from broad bottom to top. Place stuffed leaves side by side in a large stockpot, leaving no gaps (this prevents leaves from opening while cooking).

Pour remaining broth over top of leaves. Set pan over medium heat and bring to a simmer. Reduce heat to low, cover and simmer 1 hour. Remove from heat and let cool 30 minutes before serving. (Note: Stuffed grape leaves may also be served chilled.)

Serves 16

Nutrition Facts

Nutrition (per serving): 29.5 calories; 10% calories from fat; 0.4g total fat; 0.0mg cholesterol; 126.1mg sodium; 83.0mg potassium; 6.1g carbohydrates; 1.4g fiber; 1.1g sugar; 1.2g protein.

Roasted Eggplant Basil Spread

2 medium eggplants
1 1/3 cup fresh basil - (packed)
20 medium green olives, pitted
2 large garlic cloves, coarsely chopped
1 tsp table salt

Heat oven to 375 degrees. Cut eggplant in half lengthwise. Place eggplant halves, cut-side down, on a baking sheet coated with cooking spray. Roast until eggplant is soft, about 35 to 40 minutes. Cool to room temperature.

With a spoon, scrape flesh from eggplant into a food processor or blender. Add basil, olives, garlic and salt; blend until coarsely puréed. Allow to sit for at least 30 minutes before serving.

Serves 6

Nutrition Facts

Nutrition (per serving): 27.5 calories; 51% calories from fat; 1.6g total fat; 0.0mg cholesterol; 516.5mg sodium; 111.7mg potassium; 3.2g carbohydrates; 1.8g fiber; 0.7g sugar; 0.7g protein.

Roasted Eggplant Crostini

1 medium eggplant, peeled, and cut into 1" pieces
1 medium sweet red pepper, cut 1" pieces
1 medium red onion, cut 1" pieces
3 medium garlic cloves, chopped
1 1/2 tsp olive oil
1 tsp table salt
1/2 tsp freshly-ground black pepper
1 Tbs canned tomato paste
1 lb Italian bread, cut into thirty-two 1/2-oz slices, each
sliced equals 4 1/2" by 3 1/4" by 3/4"

Preheat oven to 400 degrees.

Arrange all ingredients, except tomato paste and bread slices, in the bottom of a roasting pan; mix well to coat. Roast until vegetables are tender, mixing occasionally, about 40 minutes.

Place eggplant mixture in a food processor and add tomato paste; pulse about 6 times until very small pieces form (do not puree until smooth).

Toast bread slices. Spread 1 tablespoon eggplant mixture on each bread slice and serve.

Serves 32

Nutrition Facts

Nutrition (per serving): 46.2 calories; 14% calories from fat; 0.8g total fat; 0.0mg cholesterol; 160.0mg sodium; 63.1mg potassium; 8.5g carbohydrates; 1.0g fiber; 0.7g sugar; 1.5g protein.

Shrimp Marinated In Lime and Dijon Mustard

1 medium sweet onion, sliced thin rings
1/2 cup fresh lime juice
Lime rind, as garnish
2 Tbs capers
2 Tbs Dijon mustard
1/2 tsp hot sauce
1 cup water
1/2 cup white wine vinegar
3 whole cloves
1 bay leaf
1 lb shrimp, peeled, deveined

Combine onion, lime juice, capers, mustard and hot sauce into a shallow dish. In a saucepan bring the water, vinegar, cloves and bay leaf to a boil. Add shrimp. Cook for one minute stirring constantly.

Add shrimp mixture to shallow dish containing onion mixture. Stir to combine. Cover and refrigerate. Discard cloves and bay leaf. Serve with water crackers or melba toast.

Serves 4

Nutrition Facts

Nutrition (per serving): 105.0 calories; 8% calories from fat; 1.0g total fat; 175.0mg cholesterol; 380.0mg sodium; 5.0g carbohydrates; 19.0g protein.

Southwestern Potato Skins

6 large baking potatoes
1 tsp oil
1 tsp chili powder
6 dashes Tabasco sauce
6 slices turkey bacon, chopped, crisped
1 medium tomato
2 Tbs sliced green onions
1/2 cup shredded Cheddar cheese
Salsa, (optional)

Scrub potatoes and prick with a fork. Microwave uncovered on HIGH for about 10 minutes or until tender. Cool. Halve each potato lengthwise, leaving a 1/4-inch shell. Combine oil, chili powder and hot sauce into a small bowl. Brush this mixture into the insides of the potatoes. Cut each half of each potato in half again. Place onto a baking sheet.

Fill each with chopped turkey bacon, tomato and green onion. Top with cheese. Bake in a 450 degree oven for about 10 minutes or until cheese is melted and wedges are heated through. Optionally, serve with salsa. Two tablespoons adds less than 20 calories.

Serves 6

Nutrition Facts

Nutrition (per serving): 215.0 calories; 20% calories from fat; 5.0g total fat; 10.0mg cholesterol; 185.0mg sodium; 37.0g carbohydrates; 4.0g fiber; 6.0g protein.

Stuffed Cucumber Appetizers

2 medium cucumbers
1 can unsalted water-packed tuna, drained
1/2 cup fat-free mayonnaise
1/4 cup finely-chopped celery
1 finely-chopped apple, skin on
Shredded lettuce

Cut medium-sized cucumbers in half lengthwise. Remove the seeds. In a small bowl, combine the remaining ingredients. Stuff the cucumber halves mounding to use all the tuna mixture. Wrap in cellophane or waxed paper. Chill until just before serving.

Cut into 1-inch chunks. Stand cucumber on end and serve on a bed of shredded lettuce.

Serves 16

Nutrition Facts

Nutrition (per serving): 30.0 calories; 27% calories from fat; 1.0g total fat; 3.0mg cholesterol; 3.0mg sodium; 3.0g carbohydrates; 0.5g fiber; 3.0g protein.

Tri-Color Mediterranean Salsa

1/2 tsp olive oil
1 cup diced green bell pepper
1 cup diced red bell pepper
1 cup diced yellow bell pepper
2 Tbs capers
1 garlic clove, minced
3 Tbs finely-chopped fresh basil
2 Tbs red wine vinegar
1/2 tsp dried thyme
1/2 tsp freshly-ground black pepper
1/4 tsp chopped fresh rosemary

Heat oil in a large skillet. Add peppers, capers and garlic; sauté until tender. Remove from heat; stir in basil and vinegar. Before serving add thyme and pepper.

Excellent as a topping for grilled fish. Also is excellent over grilled vegetables or as a dip for pita bread triangles.

Serves 4

Nutrition Facts

Nutrition (per serving): 25.0 calories; 23% calories from fat; 0.6g total fat; 5.0mg sodium; 4.0g carbohydrates; 1.0g fiber; 0.5g protein.

Desserts

Apple Cake

Autumn Fruit with Tofu Whipped Topping

Berries with Creamy Lemon Sauce

Brownie Cupcake Bites

Carrot Cake

Chocolate Turtle Cookies

Chocolate-Amaretto Cheesecake

Fat Free Chocolate Cake

Fruit Spread Coffee Cake

Lemon-Honey Cookies

Oatmeal-Raisin Cookies

Orange Honey Cake

Pineapple Right-Side-Up Cake

Spiced Baked Apples with Vanilla Sauce

Strawberry Sorbet

Upside-Down German Chocolate Cake

Upside-Down No-Bake Cheesecake

Watermelon Sherbet

Zabaglione

Apple Cake

3 1/3 cups all-purpose flour
1 tsp baking soda
1 tsp cinnamon
1 dash salt
1 cup sugar
4 egg whites
4 apples, cored and diced
1 1/2 cups unsweetened applesauce
2 tsp vanilla extract

Preheat the oven to 350 degrees. Spray a 10-inch tube pan with nonstick cooking spray.

In a medium bowl, combine the flour, baking soda, cinnamon and salt.

In a large bowl, with an electric mixer at high speed, beat the sugar and egg whites until soft peaks form. With the mixer at low speed, blend in the apples, applesauce and vanilla. Add the flour mixture; stir until just combined (do not over mix).

Scrape the batter into the pan; spread it smooth. Bake until golden and a toothpick inserted in the center comes out clean, about 55 minutes. Cool in the pan on a rack 10 minutes. Remove from the pan and cool on the rack 20 minutes longer; serve warm.

Serves 18

Nutrition Facts

Nutrition (per serving): 156.0 calories; 91.0mg sodium; 35.0g carbohydrates; 1.0g fiber; 3.0g protein.

Autumn Fruit with Tofu Whipped Topping

1 serving cooking spray
2 medium Granny Smith apples, cored, and chopped into 1/2" pieces
2 medium Bosc or Bartlett pears, cored, and chopped into 1/2" pieces
1/4 cup Splenda No Calorie Sweetener
1/2 tsp ground cinnamon
1/2 cups fresh or frozen cranberries
8 oz soft tofu, pressed to remove as much water as possible
1/8 cup Splenda No Calorie Sweetener
1 tsp vanilla extract
1/8 tsp ground cinnamon

Coat a nonstick skillet with cooking spray and heat over medium-high heat. Toss apples and pears with 1/4 cup of Splenda and 1/2 teaspoon of cinnamon in a medium bowl. Add fruit mixture to skillet and sauté until fruit starts to soften and brown, about 5 to 7 minutes. Add cranberries and cook 5 minutes more. Remove from heat and keep warm.

Place tofu in bowl of food processor and process until smooth, about 3 minutes. Add 1/8 cup (2 tablespoons) of Splenda, vanilla and 1/8 teaspoon of cinnamon and blend until smooth, about 3 to 5 minutes. To serve, top 1/2 cup of fruit with 1/4 cup of whipped topping.

Serves 4

Nutrition Facts

Nutrition (per serving): 186.7 calories; 11% calories from fat; 2.5g total fat; 0.0mg cholesterol; 7.2mg sodium; 256.0mg potassium; 39.1g carbohydrates; 5.2g fiber; 16.4g sugar; 4.6g protein.

Berries with Creamy Lemon Sauce

1 1/2 cups fat-free (skim) milk
1/4 cup sugar
1 Tbs all-purpose flour
3/4 tsp lemon extract
2 cups strawberries, hulled, halved
1 cup blueberries

Combine milk, sugar and flour in the top of a double boiler. Cook over simmering water, stirring frequently, until mixture thickens, about 30 minutes. Remove from heat and stir in lemon extract. Place plastic wrap on surface of mixture; refrigerate until cool.

Place about 1/2 cup of strawberries and 1/4 cup of blueberries into each of 4 stemmed glasses. Spoon about 1/3 cup of lemon sauce into each cup.

Serves 4

Nutrition Facts

Nutrition (per serving): 146.5 calories; 13% calories from fat; 2.2g total fat; 7.3mg cholesterol; 38.7mg sodium; 285.0mg potassium; 29.4g carbohydrates; 2.4g fiber; 24.3g sugar; 4.0g protein.

Brownie Cupcake Bites

21 oz regular brownie dry mix
1/2 cup water
1/2 cup unsweetened applesauce
2 large egg whites, lightly beaten
1 1/2 cups lite whipped topping
1 1/4 oz candy corn - (abt 24 pieces)

Preheat oven to 350 degrees. Line 24 mini muffin tin holes with mini cupcake papers.

Combine brownie mix, water, applesauce and egg whites in a large mixing bowl. Beat 50 strokes with a wooden spoon; do not under mix. Pour brownie mixture into prepared muffin tins.

Bake cupcakes until a tester inserted in center of a cupcake comes out clean, about 12 minutes. Remove from oven and cool completely; remove cupcakes from pan. Before serving, decorate each cooled cupcake with a tablespoon dollop of whipped topping and 1 piece of candy corn.

Serves 24

Nutrition Facts

Nutrition (per serving): 122.0 calories; 23% calories from fat; 3.3g total fat; 0.0mg cholesterol; 82.5mg sodium; 9.6mg potassium; 21.8g carbohydrates; 0.1g fiber; 12.9g sugar; 1.5g protein.

Carrot Cake

1 3/4 cups all-purpose flour
1/2 cup whole-wheat flour
2 tsp baking soda
1 tsp cinnamon
1 tsp ground allspice
1/4 tsp grated nutmeg
1/8 tsp salt
1/2 cup light brown sugar - (firmly packed)
2 egg, whites
6 carrots, shredded
2 cans crushed unsweetened pineapple - (8 oz ea), drained
2/3 cup low-fat (1%) buttermilk
1/2 cup raisins
3 Tbs canola oil
2 tsp vanilla extract
1 tsp almond extract

Preheat the oven to 350 degrees. Spray a 13- by 9-inch baking pan with nonstick cooking spray.

In a medium bowl, combine the flours, baking soda, cinnamon, allspice, nutmeg and salt.

In a large bowl, with an electric mixer at high speed, beat the sugar and egg whites until thick and frothy. With the mixer at low speed, stir in the carrots, pineapple, buttermilk, raisins, oil and the extracts. Gradually add the flour mixture and stir until all the flour is just moistened.

Scrape the batter into the pan. Bake until golden and a toothpick inserted in the center comes out clean, about 35 minutes. Cool completely in the pan on a rack.

Serves 16

Nutrition Facts

Nutrition (per serving): 159.0 calories; 16% calories from fat; 3.0g total fat; 1.0mg cholesterol; 214.0mg sodium; 31.0g carbohydrates; 2.0g fiber; 3.0g protein.

Chocolate Turtle Cookies

1 cup all-purpose flour
1/3 cup unsweetened cocoa
2/3 cup sugar
1/4 cup reduced-calorie margarine
1/4 cup fat-free cream cheese
1 large egg white
2 Tbs fat-free milk
1 tsp vanilla extract
24 caramel candies
24 pecan halves

Combine flour and cocoa in a small bowl; set aside. Beat together sugar, margarine, cream cheese, egg white, milk, and vanilla extract in a large bowl; add flour mixture and blend well. Chill dough at least 30 minutes, or until firm.

Preheat oven to 350 degrees. Lightly coat 2 baking sheets with cooking spray.

Shape dough into 1-inch balls; place on baking sheets about 1 to 2 inches apart. Press a caramel into each cookie and flatten; top each caramel with a pecan half. Bake for 10 minutes. Allow cookies to cool on baking sheets and then remove to a wire rack to cool completely.

Serves 24

Nutrition Facts

Nutrition (per serving): 109.9 calories; 30% calories from fat; 3.8g total fat; 2.8mg cholesterol; 64.4mg sodium; 56.1mg potassium; 18.5g carbohydrates; 0.8g fiber; 12.4g sugar; 1.6g protein.

Chocolate-Amaretto Cheesecake

6 chocolate graham cracker 2" squares, made into crumbs
2 1/3 cups part-skim ricotta cheese
4 oz nonfat cream cheese
1/2 cup sugar
1/4 cup unsweetened cocoa powder
1 egg
3 Tbs all-purpose flour
2 Tbs Amaretto liqueur
1 tsp vanilla extract
2 Tbs semisweet chocolate chips

Preheat the oven to 300 degrees. Spray an 8-inch springform pan with nonstick cooking spray. Sprinkle the cracker crumbs evenly over the bottom of the pan.

In a blender or food processor, puree the ricotta and cream cheeses, the sugar, cocoa, egg, flour, liqueur and vanilla; stir in the chocolate chips.

Pour the cheese mixture over the crumbs. Bake until a knife inserted in the center comes out clean, about 1 1/2 hours. Cool completely on a rack. Refrigerate, covered, until chilled, at least 3 hours.

Serves 12

Nutrition Facts

Nutrition (per serving): 99.0 calories; 18% calories from fat; 2.0g total fat; 21.0mg cholesterol; 82.0mg sodium; 17.0g carbohydrates; 1.0g fiber; 3.0g protein.

Fat Free Chocolate Cake

3 1/3 cups all-purpose flour
1/2 cup unsweetened cocoa powder, sifted
1 1/2 tsp baking soda
1/2 tsp salt
1 1/2 cups granulated sugar
1/2 cup plain nonfat yogurt
2 egg whites
1 Tbs vanilla extract
1 Tbs white vinegar
2 Tbs confectioners' sugar

Preheat the oven to 350 degrees. Spray a 13- by 9-inch baking pan with nonstick cooking spray.

In a medium bowl, combine the flour, cocoa, baking soda and salt.

In a large bowl, with an electric mixer at medium speed, beat the granulated sugar, yogurt, egg whites, vanilla and vinegar until fluffy, about 2 minutes. With the mixer at low speed, gradually add the flour mixture; stir until just combined (do not over mix). Add 2 cups water and stir until just smooth.

Pour the batter into the pan. Bake until a toothpick inserted in the center comes out clean, about 40 minutes. Cool completely in the pan on a rack. Dust with the confectioners' sugar.

Serves 24

Nutrition Facts

Nutrition (per serving): 124.0 calories; 133.0mg sodium; 28.0g carbohydrates; 1.0g fiber; 3.0g protein.

Fruit Spread Coffee Cake

3 1/3 cups reduced-fat buttermilk baking mix
1/2 cup granulated sugar
3 Tbs cold unsalted stick margarine, diced
2/3 cup fat-free egg substitute
1/2 cup skim milk
1 tsp vanilla extract
1/2 tsp almond extract
1 cup spreadable fruit (any flavor)
1/2 cup confectioners' sugar

Preheat the oven to 350 degrees. Spray a 15- by 10-inch jelly-roll pan with nonstick cooking spray.

In a large bowl, combine the baking mix and granulated sugar. With a pastry blender or 2 knives, cut in the margarine until the mixture resembles coarse crumbs. Add the egg substitute, milk, and the extracts; with a wooden spoon, stir until just combined (do not over mix).

Spread two-thirds of the batter into the pan, smoothing the top; spoon the spreadable fruit evenly over the batter. Drop the remaining batter by tablespoonfuls evenly over the fruit. Bake until light brown and a toothpick inserted in the center comes out clean, about 25 minutes. Cool in the pan on a rack 10 minutes.

Meanwhile, whisk the confectioners' sugar with 1 tablespoon water until smooth; drizzle evenly over the top of the cake while it is still warm.

Serves 18

Nutrition Facts

Nutrition (per serving): 175.0 calories; 15% calories from fat; 3.0g total fat; 263.0mg sodium; 33.0g carbohydrates; 3.0g protein.

Lemon-Honey Cookies

1/2 cup margarine
3/4 cup sugar
1 tsp lemon zest
1 tsp baking powder
1/4 tsp baking soda
2 large egg whites
1/3 cup fat-free skim milk
1 Tbs fresh lemon juice
1 3/4 cups all-purpose flour
2 Tbs honey
3 Tbs powdered sugar

Preheat oven to 350 degrees.

In a large mixing bowl, beat margarine with an electric mixer on medium-high speed for 30 seconds. Add sugar, zest, baking powder and baking soda; beat until combined, scraping sides of bowl occasionally. Add egg whites, milk and lemon juice; beat until combined. Beat in as much of the flour as you can with the mixer and then stir in remaining flour by hand.

Drop dough by rounded teaspoonfuls, 2 inches apart, onto 2 ungreased cookie sheets. Bake until edges are lightly browned, about 12 minutes. Transfer cookies to a wire rack and let cool. Repeat with remaining cookie dough.

Brush tops of each cookie with a touch of honey just before serving and then sprinkle with powdered sugar; stack in a single layer to prevent sticking.

Serves 24

Nutrition Facts

Nutrition (per serving): 105.9 calories; 32% calories from fat; 3.9g total fat; 4.2mg cholesterol; 61.8mg sodium; 24.5mg potassium; 16.6g carbohydrates; 0.3g fiber; 9.5g sugar; 1.4g protein.

Oatmeal-Raisin Cookies

1 3/4 cups quick-cooking oatmeal
1 cup all-purpose flour
2 Tbs nonfat dry milk
1 tsp baking powder
1 tsp cinnamon
1/4 tsp salt
1/2 cup light brown sugar - (firmly packed)
1/4 cup unsalted stick margarine
1 egg white
1/2 cup skim milk
3/4 cup raisins
1 tsp vanilla

Arrange the oven racks to divide the oven into thirds; preheat the oven to 375 degrees. Spray 2 nonstick baking sheets with nonstick cooking spray.

In a large bowl, combine the oatmeal, flour, dry milk, baking powder, cinnamon and salt.

In another large bowl, with an electric mixer at high speed, beat the sugar, margarine and egg white until light and fluffy. With the mixer at low speed, alternately add the skim milk and the flour mixture with the raisins and vanilla; stir until just combined (do not over mix).

Drop the dough by tablespoons onto the baking sheets, making 24 cookies. Bake until golden, about 15 minutes. Cool completely on a rack; store in an airtight container for 3 to 4 days.

Serves 24

Nutrition Facts

Nutrition (per serving): 95.0 calories; 19% calories from fat; 2.0g total fat; 52.0mg sodium; 17.0g carbohydrates; 1.0g fiber; 2.0g protein.

Orange Honey Cake

1 serving cooking spray
2/3 cup honey
1/3 cup sugar
2 large eggs
1/4 cup reduced-calorie margarine, soft
2 1/4 cups all-purpose flour
1 tsp baking powder
1/2 tsp baking soda
1 tsp ground cinnamon
1/4 tsp table salt
1/4 cup black coffee, strong
1/2 cup chopped walnuts - (abt 2 1/4 oz)
2 Tbs orange zest

Preheat oven to 325 degrees. Spray an 8-inch round baking pan with cooking spray and then line with wax paper.

In a large bowl, combine honey, sugar, eggs and margarine; mix well.

In another large bowl, combine flour, baking powder, baking soda, cinnamon and salt. Stir half of flour mixture into honey mixture and then stir in coffee; mix well. Add honey mixture back to remaining flour mixture and stir in walnuts and orange zest; mix well.

Bake until a knife inserted into center of cake comes out clean, about 30 minutes. Cool on a wire rack before slicing into 12 pieces.

Serves 12

Nutrition Facts

Nutrition (per serving): 229.8 calories; 23% calories from fat; 6.3g total fat; 40.9mg cholesterol; 163.6mg sodium; 87.2mg potassium; 40.3g carbohydrates; 1.2g fiber; 21.3g sugar; 4.5g protein.

Pineapple Right-Side-Up Cake

1/2 cup unsweetened applesauce
1 can unsweetened crushed pineapple - (8 oz),
drained
= (reserve the juice)
1/3 cup skim milk
1/3 cup fat-free egg substitute
1/2 tsp vanilla extract
1 3/4 cups all-purpose flour
1/3 cup granulated sugar
2 tsp double-acting baking powder
1/4 cup light brown sugar - (firmly packed)

Preheat the oven to 350 degrees. Spray a 9-inch square baking pan with nonstick cooking spray.

In a medium bowl, with a wooden spoon, stir together the applesauce, pineapple juice, milk, egg substitute and vanilla.

In a large bowl, combine the flour, granulated sugar and baking powder; make a well in the center. Add the applesauce mixture; stir until just combined (do not over mix).

Scrape the batter into the pan. Spoon the crushed pineapple over the batter and sprinkle with the brown sugar. Bake until golden and a toothpick inserted in the center comes out clean, about 30 minutes. Cool in the pan on a rack 10 minutes; serve warm.

Serves 12

Nutrition Facts

Nutrition (per serving): 124.0 calories; 98.0mg sodium; 28.0g carbohydrates; 1.0g fiber; 3.0g protein.

Spiced Baked Apples with Vanilla Sauce

4 medium apples, cored
1 tsp ground cinnamon
1/2 tsp ground ginger
12 tsp Splenda No Calorie Sweetener
1/4 cup water
2 Tbs fresh lemon juice
1 oz fat-free sugar-free instant vanilla pudding mix
3/4 cup fat-free skim milk

Preheat oven to 350 degrees. Using a vegetable peeler, peel a 1/2-inch horizontal strip around apples to help release juices during baking. Place apples in a 9- by 9-inch baking dish.

Combine cinnamon, ginger and Splenda in a small bowl. Place 1 tablespoon of cinnamon mixture in cored-out center of each apple, then sprinkle with remaining cinnamon mixture. Combine water and lemon juice in a cup. Pour liquid around apples.

Bake until apples are soft when pierced with a knife, about 15 to 20 minutes. Remove from oven and let cool.

Pour pudding mix into a medium bowl. Whisk in milk to make a fairly thin sauce. Place one apple on a plate and drizzle with sauce.

Serves 4

Nutrition Facts

Nutrition (per serving): 134.5 calories; 1% calories from fat; 0.3g total fat; 1.0mg cholesterol; 36.7mg sodium; 238.0mg potassium; 33.1g carbohydrates; 3.7g fiber; 18.0g sugar; 2.3g protein.

Strawberry Sorbet

6 cups strawberries, hulled and washed
1/2 cup superfine sugar
1/4 cup fresh lemon juice
2 Tbs strawberry liqueur
Mint sprigs

In a food processor or blender, puree the strawberries, sugar, lemon juice and liqueur. Pour the mixture into a 12- by 8-inch glass baking dish; freeze, covered, until the mixture is frozen 1-inch around the edges, about 2 hours.

With a whisk, beat the mixture to break up the large frozen crystals, 1 to 2 minutes. Return to the freezer and freeze, covered, until firm, at least 3 hours.

Soften in the refrigerator 20 minutes and serve, garnished with the mint sprigs.

Serves 8

Nutrition Facts

Nutrition (per serving): 95.0 calories; 1.0mg sodium; 22.0g carbohydrates; 3.0g fiber; 1.0g protein.

Upside-Down German Chocolate Cake

1 serving cooking spray = (5 one-second sprays per serving)
2 Tbs light butter
3/4 cup water
2/3 cup brown sugar - (unpacked)
3/4 cup packaged shredded coconut
1/2 cup chopped pecans
5 large egg whites
1 cup buttermilk
1/2 cup fat-free sour cream
1/3 cup unsweetened applesauce
18 1/2 oz German chocolate cake mix - (1 pkg)

Preheat oven to 350 degrees. Coat a 9- by 13-inch nonstick baking pan with cooking spray.

In a small saucepan over low heat, melt butter with water. Stir in brown sugar until smooth; pour evenly into baking pan. Sprinkle coconut and pecans evenly over melted sugar mixture.

In a large bowl, using an electric mixer set on high speed, beat egg whites for 30 seconds. Beat in buttermilk, sour cream and applesauce. Add cake mix and beat on low speed until moistened, about 30 seconds. Beat for an additional 2 minutes; pour into pan.

Bake for 40 minutes. Cool in pan on a rack. Cut into 16 pieces and serve.

Serves 16

Nutrition Facts

Nutrition (per serving): 217.4 calories; 33% calories from fat; 8.5g total fat; 0.1mg cholesterol; 413.4mg sodium; 114.1mg potassium; 34.0g carbohydrates; 1.9g fiber; 17.9g sugar; 3.5g protein.

Upside-Down No-Bake Cheesecake

1 Tbs fresh lemon juice
1 envelope unflavored gelatin
1/2 cup evaporated skimmed milk
1/4 cup sugar
2 cups nonfat cottage cheese
1 cup aspartame-sweetened vanilla nonfat yogurt
2 Tbs nonfat sour cream
1 tsp vanilla extract
1/8 tsp almond extract
12 graham cracker 2 1/2" squares, made into crumbs
1 1/2 cups fresh raspberries (or 1 1/2 cups sliced fresh
strawberries)

In a small bowl, combine the lemon juice and 2 tablespoons cold water; sprinkle with the gelatin and let soften 5 minutes.

Meanwhile, in a small saucepan over medium heat, heat the milk and sugar until the sugar is dissolved and the milk is just heated through, 2 to 3 minutes. Remove from the heat and stir in the gelatin mixture, stirring until the gelatin is thoroughly dissolved.

In a blender or food processor, puree the cottage cheese, yogurt, sour cream, extracts and the gelatin mixture. Pour into a 10- by 6-inch glass baking dish; sprinkle evenly with the cracker crumbs. Refrigerate, covered, until firm, at least 3 hours. Top with the raspberries.

Serves 8

Nutrition Facts

Nutrition (per serving): 158.0 calories; 5% calories from fat; 1.0g total fat; 6.0mg cholesterol; 303.0mg sodium; 25.0g carbohydrates; 1.0g fiber; 11.0g protein.

Watermelon Sherbet

8 cups watermelon, chopped and seeded
1 1/2 Tbs lime juice
1 cup light honey
1/2 tsp ground cardamom
1/2 package unflavored gelatin
1/2 cup nonfat plain yogurt
12 mint leaves

Place watermelon and lime juice in a blender and puree. Set a colander or sieve over a large bowl and pour pureed watermelon through sieve, separating juice from pulp. Place juice, honey, cardamom, and gelatin in a large saucepan over medium-high heat. Cook just to boiling point, then remove from heat. Let cool. Pour into a shallow pan or ice cube tray and freeze to slush point (about 1-1/2 hours).

Whisk yogurt into watermelon slush, then return to freezer. Allow to freeze solid (about 2 hours). Stir every hour to break up ice crystals.

To serve, cut sherbet into large chunks and puree very briefly in a blender or food processor. Spoon into dessert glasses, garnish with mint leaf, and serve.

Serves 12

Nutrition Facts

Nutrition (per serving): 139.6 calories; 2% calories from fat; 0.3g total fat; 0.6mg cholesterol; 26.9mg sodium; 175.2mg potassium; 35.6g carbohydrates; 0.8g fiber; 32.8g sugar; 1.7g protein.

Zabaglione

5 egg yolks
1/2 cup superfine sugar
2/3 cup Marsala wine or sweet sherry
fresh fruit or amaretti cookies, to serve (optional)

Place the egg yolks in a heatproof bowl. Add the sugar to the egg yolks and whisk until the mixture is thick and very pale and has doubled in volume.

Place the bowl containing the egg mixture over a pan of simmering water,

Add the Marsala to the egg mixture and continue whisking until the mixture becomes warm and foamy. This process may take as long as 10 minutes.

Pour the mixture, which should now be foamy and light, into 4 wine glasses.

Serve the mousse warm with fresh fruit or amaretti cookies, if you like.

Serves 4

Preparation time: 5 minutes

Cooking time: 10 minutes

Nutrition Facts

Nutrition (per serving): 158.0 calories; 6% calories from fat; 1.0g total fat; 29.0g carbohydrates; 29.0g sugar; 1.0g protein.

Entrees

Apple Stuffed Tenderloin with Cinnamon Raisin Sauce
Baja-Style Fish Tacos with Salad and Chili-Lime Sauce
Beef Stroganoff
Buffalo Chicken Fingers
Cheddar Baked Chicken with Mushrooms
Chicken Fajitas
Chicken Fingers with Ranch Dip and Seasoned Fries
Chicken Kebabs
Chicken Tetrazzini
Chicken Tostadas
Cod with Lemon and Capers
'Fried' Fish Sandwich
Garden Vegetable Wraps
Garlic Scampi
Grilled Swordfish with Seasoned Asparagus
Grilled Tuna with Fresh Tomato Salsa
Heart-Healthy Vegetable Pasta
Hush Puppy Chicken Casserole
Lamb-Vegetable Kabobs
Loose Beef Fajitas
Mexican Beef and Cheese Wontons with Salsa
Moo Shu Beef Lettuce Cups
Orange Beef Stir-Fry
Orange Rosemary Roasted Chicken
Roasted and Stuffed Smothered Eggplant
Salmon Burgers with Peach Salsa
Savory Beef Burgers
Scallops with Red Pepper Sauce
Thai Stir-Fry Chicken
Tomato and Tarragon Braised Sole
Turkey Cordon Bleu

Apple Stuffed Tenderloin with Cinnamon Raisin Sauce

=== STUFFED TENDERLOIN ===
1 1/2 lbs pork tenderloin, trimmed of all visible fat
2 medium oranges
1 medium apple, cored, chopped
2 Tbs finely-chopped onions
2/3 cup fine dry plain bread crumbs

=== SAUCE ===
1 cup unsweetened apple juice
1 Tbs cornstarch
1/4 tsp ground cinnamon
1/4 cup raisins

To make the stuffed pork tenderloin: Preheat the oven to 425 degrees. Cut a pocket in the side of the tenderloin by cutting a lengthwise slit from one side to almost the other side and stopping about 1/2 inch from each of the tapered ends. Set the tenderloin aside.

Finely shred the peel from the oranges and set aside. Then squeeze 3 tablespoons of juice from the oranges. In a medium bowl, combine the orange juice and apples. Set the apple mixture aside.

Spray an unheated small skillet with no-stick spray. Add the onions. Cook and stir over medium heat until tender. Then add the onions and bread crumbs to the apple mixture. Toss until combined.

Spoon the bread mixture into the pocket of the tenderloin. Securely close the pocket with wooden toothpicks. Place the tenderloin on a rack in a shallow roasting pan. Insert a meat thermometer into the meat portion only. Bake for 25 to 30 minutes or until the thermometer registers 160 degrees. Let stand about 5 minutes before slicing.

To make the sauce: In a small saucepan, use a wire whisk to stir together 2 tablespoons of the apple juice and the cornstarch. Then stir in the remaining apple juice. Cook and stir over medium heat until boiling. Stir in the reserved orange peel and cinnamon. Add the raisins and cook for 5 minutes, stirring occasionally.

To serve, slice the tenderloin. Spoon the sauce over the slices.

Serves 4

Nutrition Facts

Nutrition (per serving): 245.0 calories; 14% calories from fat; 4.0g total fat; 74.0mg cholesterol; 4.2g fiber.

Baja-Style Fish Tacos with Salad and Chili-Lime Sauce

2 servings cooking spray
1/2 cup yellow masa corn flour
1 tsp table salt
1/4 tsp freshly-ground black pepper
1/8 tsp cayenne pepper
1/4 tsp garlic powder
1/2 tsp paprika
1 lb red snapper fillets,, cut 2" pieces
8 medium corn tortillas, buy a few extra in case some break
1 head romaine lettuce, outer leaves removed and remaining leaves sliced into 1/4" strips
5 medium red radishes, thinly sliced
2 medium scallions, thinly sliced
10 medium cherry tomatoes, quartered
1/4 cup shredded red cabbage
3/4 cup low-fat plain yogurt
2 Tbs fresh lime juice
1 tsp canned chipotle peppers in adobo sauce, finely chopped
2 Tbs fresh cilantro sprigs, for garnish

Preheat broiler to high. Line a baking sheet with aluminum foil (or nonstick aluminum foil) and coat with cooking spray (helps to make fish crispy).

Place corn flour, salt, black pepper, cayenne pepper, garlic powder and paprika in a large bowl; mix to combine. Add snapper to corn flour mixture and toss to coat

Place seasoned fish on prepared baking sheet and lightly coat tops of fish with cooking spray. Broil until crispy, about 3 to 4 minutes per side.

Meanwhile, wrap tortillas in aluminum foil and place in oven to warm; place on rack furthest from heat source.

To make salad, combine lettuce, radishes, scallions, tomatoes and cabbage in a medium bowl; set aside.

To make sauce, combine yogurt, lime juice and chipotle peppers in a blender; blend until smooth.

To assemble, place a tortilla on a plate. Top with 2 to 3 pieces of fish, 1/2 cup of salad and 2 tablespoons of sauce; roll up and repeat with remaining ingredients.

This recipe yields 4 servings; 2 filled tortillas per serving.

Serves 4

Nutrition Facts

Nutrition (per serving): 361.1 calories; 12% calories from fat; 5.1g total fat; 44.8mg cholesterol; 739.9mg sodium; 1289.8mg potassium; 48.4g carbohydrates; 7.4g fiber; 2.6g sugar; 32.8g protein.

Beef Stroganoff

=== SAUCE ===
1 cup evaporated skim milk
1 Tbs cornstarch
1 envelope instant onion-mushroom soup dip mix
=== BEEF MIXTURE ===
12 oz beef sirloin steak, trimmed of all
visible fat and cut thin bite-sized strips
1/2 medium onion, sliced, and
separated into rings
1 garlic clove, minced
1 1/2 cups sliced fresh mushrooms
1 container fat-free plain yogurt - (8 oz)
2 cups hot cooked noodles
Fresh parsley, (optional)

To make the sauce: In a medium saucepan, use a wire whisk to stir together the milk and cornstarch until smooth. Then stir in the soup mix. Bring to a boil over medium heat, stirring constantly. Remove from the heat. Cover to keep warm.

To make the beef mixture: Lightly spray an unheated large skillet with no-stick spray. Add the beef, onions and garlic. Cook and stir over medium-high heat for 2 minutes. Add the mushrooms. Cook and stir about 1 minute more or until the onions and mushrooms are tender.

Reduce the heat to low. Stir the sauce mixture into the beef mixture. Then stir in the yogurt. Cook and stir just until heated through. (Do not overheat because the yogurt will curdle.)

Serve over the hot noodles. If desired, top with the parsley to garnish.

Serves 4

Nutrition Facts

Nutrition (per serving): 398.0 calories; 20% calories from fat; 9.0g total fat; 69.0mg cholesterol; 2.1g fiber.

Buffalo Chicken Fingers

1 serving cooking spray
1 1/4 lbs uncooked boneless skinless chicken breast, cut
16 strips total
1/2 tsp table salt
1/2 tsp paprika
1 tsp minced garlic
2 Tbs fat-free margarine
4 tsp hot pepper sauce, or to taste
1/2 cup fat-free blue cheese dressing
4 medium celery stalks, trimmed, and cut into 4 sticks
each

Coat a large nonstick skillet with cooking spray and heat over medium-high heat.

Place chicken on a plate and sprinkle with salt and paprika. Add chicken to skillet and cook, turning occasionally until lightly browned and cooked through, about 5 to 7 minutes. Add garlic; reduce heat to low, stir and cook until fragrant, about 30 seconds.

Remove skillet from heat; stir in margarine and hot sauce until margarine melts. Serve chicken with blue cheese dressing and celery on the side.

Serves 4

Nutrition Facts

Nutrition (per serving): 164.9 calories; 11% calories from fat; 2.1g total fat; 13.9mg cholesterol; 1280.9mg sodium; 1908.3mg potassium; 29.5g carbohydrates; 12.1g fiber; 19.7g sugar; 10.6g protein.

Cheddar Baked Chicken with Mushrooms

4 boneless skinless chicken breast halves
1/4 tsp freshly-ground black pepper
1 cup sliced mushrooms
1 cup grated Cheddar cheese - (4 oz)
1 1/2 cups skim milk
2 cups plain bread cubes

Preheat oven to 350 degrees. Spray baking dish with nonstick spray. Place chicken into the dish and sprinkle with pepper. Top with mushrooms, grated cheese and skim milk. Sprinkle with the bread dressing. Bake for 40 minutes.

Serves 4

Nutrition Facts

Nutrition (per serving): 370.0 calories; 31% calories from fat; 13.0g total fat; 110.0mg cholesterol; 400.0mg sodium; 28.0g carbohydrates; 35.0g protein.

Chicken Fajitas

8 medium fat-free flour tortillas
2 tsp olive oil
1 lb marinated chicken breast strips
1 lb frozen peppers and onions
1/2 cup fat-free sour cream
1/2 cup salsa

Preheat oven to 300 degrees.

Wrap tortillas in foil. Bake until warm, about 10 minutes.

Meanwhile, heat oil in a large skillet over medium-high heat. Add chicken and sauté until cooked through, stirring frequently, about 3 to 5 minutes. Transfer chicken to a serving plate, cover with foil and transfer to oven to keep warm.

In same skillet over medium-high heat, sauté frozen vegetables until tender-crisp, about 3 minutes. Serve chicken and vegetables with warm tortillas, sour cream and salsa.

Serves 4

Nutrition Facts

Nutrition (per serving): 309.1 calories; 32% calories from fat; 11.3g total fat; 22.1mg cholesterol; 897.5mg sodium; 361.3mg potassium; 40.6g carbohydrates; 2.5g fiber; 2.3g sugar; 11.9g protein.

Chicken Fingers with Ranch Dip and Seasoned Fries

3 servings cooking spray
1 lb uncooked boneless skinless chicken breasts, cut into strips
1 Tbs Dijon mustard
2 1/2 packets uncooked instant oatmeal - (1 oz ea), about 1 cup total
2 tsp garlic herb seasoning
1/2 tsp table salt
1/4 tsp freshly-ground black pepper
2 large Russet potatoes, peeled, and cut into
   1/2"-thick fries
1 Tbs Creole seasoning
1/2 cup fat-free ranch salad dressing

Preheat oven to 400 degrees. Coat a large baking sheet with cooking spray.

Coat chicken strips with mustard. Combine oats, garlic-herb seasoning, salt and pepper in a shallow dish. Dip chicken strips in oat mixture and turn to coat. Place chicken strips on prepared pan.

Arrange potatoes around chicken on pan. Lightly coat potatoes and chicken with cooking spray. Sprinkle potatoes with Creole seasoning.

Bake until chicken is cooked through and both chicken and potatoes are tender and golden brown, about 30 minutes. Serve chicken and potatoes with dressing on the side. (Note: Consider using reduced-fat or regular dressing if serving to young children.)

Serves 4

Nutrition Facts

Nutrition (per serving): 249.2 calories; 8% calories from fat; 2.5g total fat; 10.5mg cholesterol; 587.4mg sodium; 897.3mg potassium; 48.2g carbohydrates; 4.7g fiber; 1.6g sugar; 10.9g protein.

Chicken Kebabs

3/4 cup low-sodium teriyaki marinade
1/2 cup sliced green onions
2 Tbs peeled and grated ginger root
2 Tbs dark sesame oil
2 garlic cloves, minced
1 lb skinless boneless chicken breast, cut 24 pieces
8 large green onions
2 medium zucchini, cut 24 pieces
2 large bell peppers, cut 24 (1") squares
24 small button mushrooms - (abt 3/4 lb)
3 cups hot cooked rice

Combine the first 6 ingredients in a bowl; marinate in refrigerator 30 minutes, stirring occasionally.

Remove the green tops from large onions and cut white portion of each onion into 3 pieces; set aside.

Drain the chicken. Tightly thread 3 chicken pieces, 3 onion pieces, 3 zucchini pieces, 3 pepper squares and 3 mushrooms alternately onto each of 8 skewers. (If using wood skewers, soak in water for a few minutes before threading with vegetables and meat).

Place the kebabs on the barbecue and cook until done, turning frequently (about 15 to 18 minutes). Serve over rice or noodles.

Serves 4

Nutrition Facts

Nutrition (per serving): 410.0 calories; 15% calories from fat; 7.0g total fat; 72.0mg cholesterol; 48.0g carbohydrates; 3.0g fiber.

Chicken Tetrazzini

12 oz uncooked whole-wheat pasta
2 Tbs fat-free margarine, divided
3 Tbs tarragon-flavored vinegar
1 lb mushrooms, sliced (abt 6 cups)
1 1/2 cups fat-free chicken broth
1 cup fat-free skim milk
4 tsp arrowroot powder
1 tsp dried thyme
1 tsp dried tarragon
1/2 tsp table salt, or more to taste
1/4 tsp freshly-ground black pepper, or more to taste
1/4 cup fat-free sour cream
3 cups cooked chicken breast, cut bite sized
1 cup frozen peas and carrots, thawed
3 Tbs Kraft Non-Fat Grated Cheese Topping, or other brand
1 Spray of Non Stick Cooking Oil

Cook noodles according to package directions with added salt; drain and set aside.

Preheat oven to 375 degrees. Coat a 9- by 13-inch pan with cooking spray.

Heat 1 tablespoon of margarine and vinegar together in a large nonstick skillet over medium heat. Add mushrooms; cook until soft, stirring, about 5 minutes. Remove mushrooms and set aside.

Whisk broth, milk and arrowroot together in a medium-size saucepan until smooth. Stir in remaining tablespoon of margarine; set over medium heat. Cook, stirring with a wooden spoon, until thickened and boiling, about 8 minutes. Stir in thyme, tarragon, salt and pepper. Remove sauce from heat; stir in sour cream.

Combine cooked noodles, chicken, mushrooms, peas and carrots, and sauce together in a large bowl. Pour into prepared pan; sprinkle with grated topping. Bake until bubbling and hot, and top is starting to brown, about 20 minutes. Slice into 8 pieces and serve.

Serves 8

Nutrition Facts

Nutrition (per serving): 258.9 calories; 6% calories from fat; 2.0g total fat; 26.4mg cholesterol; 402.7mg sodium; 471.1mg potassium; 40.6g carbohydrates; 2.5g fiber; 3.7g sugar; 19.3g protein.

Chicken Tostadas

1 1/2 lbs cooked chicken breasts
3 cups shredded romaine lettuce
1/2 cup chopped green pepper
1/2 cup chopped tomatoes
6 flour tortillas - (6" dia)
6 Tbs fat-free sour cream
6 Tbs salsa
6 Tbs fat-free cheddar or jack cheese

Combine the chicken, lettuce, peppers, tomatoes, and onions in a large bowl.

Heat the tortillas by placing them one at a time in a dry skillet and turn once until golden and puffy.

To assemble the tostadas, place a tortilla on a plate, top with some of the chicken mixture and garnish with sour cream, salsa, and cheese. Repeat with all tortillas.

Serves 6

Nutrition Facts

Nutrition (per serving): 292.0 calories; 19% calories from fat; 6.0g total fat; 76.0mg cholesterol; 308.0mg sodium; 23.0g carbohydrates; 3.0g fiber; 4.0g sugar; 33.0g protein.

Cod with Lemon and Capers

2 lemons
4 Tbs butter
4 cod fillets - (8 oz ea)
1/2 cup large capers, drained
Non-stick cooking spray

Spray foil with non-stick spray. Place cod fillets onto foil. Squeeze the juice from one lemon over the fish. Cut the lemon into slices, place over the fish and seal the foil. Place in oven and bake at 350 degrees for about 20 minutes.

In the meantime, remove the peel from the second lemon. (Take care to cut only the peel and not the pith.) Cut into 1/4-inch wide strips. Melt the butter in a heavy saucepan over moderate heat. Add lemon peel and capers -- sauté till crispy. Serve over the fish.

Serves 4

Nutrition Facts

Nutrition (per serving): 155.0 calories; 29% calories from fat; 5.0g total fat; 60.0mg cholesterol; 350.0mg sodium; 6.0g carbohydrates; 21.0g protein.

'Fried' Fish Sandwich

1 1/4 lbs lingcod fillets - (four 5 oz pieces)
1/4 cup Dijon mustard
1/2 cup Italian-style seasoned bread crumbs
4 servings olive oil cooking spray = (or enough to coat fish)
4 medium mixed-grain hamburger rolls
8 pieces lettuce
1 small tomato, sliced

Preheat oven to 400 degrees. Coat a large baking sheet with olive oil cooking spray.

Coat both sides of each cod fillet with mustard and then bread crumbs. Arrange fillets on baking sheet and spray surface with cooking spray. Bake until fish is fork-tender and coating is golden brown, about 20 minutes.

Place fish on rolls and top each with lettuce leaves and tomato slices.

Serves 4

Nutrition Facts

Nutrition (per serving): 515.8 calories; 15% calories from fat; 9.6g total fat; 0.2mg cholesterol; 833.2mg sodium; 3865.9mg potassium; 72.2g carbohydrates; 29.2g fiber; 18.9g sugar; 47.9g protein.

Garden Vegetable Wraps

1 small zucchini, sliced
1 small sweet red pepper, chopped
1/4 cup canned black beans, rinsed, drained
1/4 cup salsa
1/4 cup low-fat shredded cheddar cheese
4 large burrito-size wheat-flour tortillas,
warmed if desired

Place zucchini, pepper and 2 tablespoons of water in a large nonstick skillet; cook over medium-high heat until crisp-tender, about 4 minutes. Stir in beans and salsa; heat through, about 1 to 2 minutes.

Spoon about 1/2 cup of mixture onto each tortilla and top each with 1 tablespoon cheese. Fold ends of tortillas in, roll and serve.

Serves 4

Nutrition Facts

Nutrition (per serving): 153.3 calories; 19% calories from fat; 3.4g total fat; 1.7mg cholesterol; 385.3mg sodium; 415.6mg potassium; 24.7g carbohydrates; 3.7g fiber; 3.8g sugar; 7.1g protein.

Garlic Scampi

3 Tbs chicken broth, defatted
2 Tbs white wine, dry sherry or
nonalcoholic white wine
1 1/2 Tbs olive oil
1/2 tsp salt
1/2 tsp dried oregano
1/4 tsp freshly-ground black pepper
3 garlic cloves, minced
1 1/2 lbs jumbo shrimp, peeled, deveined
2 lemons, cut into wedges

In a large shallow dish, stir together the broth, wine or sherry, olive oil, salt, oregano, pepper and garlic. Add the shrimp and turn them to coat them well. Cover with plastic wrap. Marinate in the refrigerator for 1 1/2 to 2 hours. (Do not marinate for longer than 2 hours or shrimp will become tough.)
Preheat the broiler. Remove the shrimp from the dish, reserving the marinade. Thread the shrimp onto skewers, leaving a small space between each.
Brush the shrimp with the reserved marinade. Broil 4 inches from the heat for 2 minutes. Turn the shrimp over, brush with the marinade and broil for 1 to 3 minutes more or until the shrimp are no longer pink.
These shrimp also are delicious grilled. Grill them directly over medium-hot coals for about 5 minutes, or until they are no longer pink.
Serve with the lemon wedges.

Serves 4

Nutrition Facts

Nutrition (per serving): 223.0 calories; 28% calories from fat; 7.0g total fat; 332.0mg cholesterol; 594.0mg sodium; 0.4g fiber.

Grilled Swordfish with Seasoned Asparagus

2 Tbs soy sauce
2 Tbs fresh lime juice
2 Tbs olive oil, divided
1 Tbs canned tomato paste
1 Tbs chopped fresh parsley
1 medium garlic clove, minced
1/2 tsp dried oregano
1/4 tsp freshly-ground black pepper
1 1/2 lbs swordfish steaks - (four 6 oz steaks)
1 lb asparagus, trimmed
1/8 tsp table salt, or to taste
1/8 tsp lemon pepper seasoning, or to taste

Combine soy sauce, lime juice, 1 tablespoon of oil, tomato paste, parsley, garlic, oregano and black pepper together in a small bowl. Place fish in a glass dish; pour soy sauce mixture over fish. Marinate fish in refrigerator for 30 minutes and then turn fish over; marinate for 30 minutes more.

Preheat grill to medium. Place asparagus in a large bowl; drizzle with remaining tablespoon of oil and season to taste with salt and lemon pepper seasoning.

Place a large piece of aluminum foil on a flat surface. Wrap asparagus in foil and grill asparagus for 30 minutes. (Or place asparagus in a pan, cover and cook on grill.) Add fish to grill after asparagus has cooked for about 15 to 20 minutes. Cook fish until it easily breaks apart with fork, flipping once, about 10 to 14 minutes total; serve immediately.

Serves 4

Nutrition Facts

Nutrition (per serving): 300.6 calories; 40% calories from fat; 13.8g total fat; 66.3mg cholesterol; 561.4mg sodium; 798.8mg potassium; 7.1g carbohydrates; 2.8g fiber; 2.9g sugar; 37.0g protein.

Grilled Tuna with Fresh Tomato Salsa

1 serving cooking spray
20 oz bluefin tuna, cut four 5-oz steaks
2 cups cherry tomatoes or grape tomatoes, halved
1 medium red onion, chopped
1/4 cup chopped parsley
1 Tbs capers
1 Tbs lemon zest
1 Tbs fresh lemon juice
1/4 tsp table salt
1/4 tsp freshly-ground black pepper

Heat a grill pan or a grill coated with cooking spray over high heat. Cook tuna, turning once, until just cooked through, about 6 minutes. (Note: For rare tuna, cook for less time, if desired.)

Meanwhile, in small bowl, combine remaining ingredients.

This recipe yields 4 servings; about one piece of tuna plus 3/4 cup of salsa per serving.

Serves 4

Nutrition Facts

Nutrition (per serving): 179.9 calories; 8% calories from fat; 1.8g total fat; 63.8mg cholesterol; 271.2mg sodium; 832.3mg potassium; 5.7g carbohydrates; 1.5g fiber; 0.2g sugar; 34.1g protein.

Heart-Healthy Vegetable Pasta

1 cup broccoli in bite-size pieces
1 cup carrots in bite-size pieces
1/4 cup chopped green onions
1/2 Tbs Italian seasoning
1 can stewed tomatoes - (14 1/2 oz), not drained
2 cups eggless spaghetti noodles
2 Tbs dry sherry wine
2 garlic cloves, minced
2 tsp grated Parmesan cheese

Cook spaghetti according to package instructions (do not add oil or salt) and drain well.

Coat a pan with non-stick cooking spray and cook broccoli, carrots and onions for 3 to 4 minutes. Add wine, garlic, seasoning and tomatoes and cook until thoroughly heated.

Pour vegetable sauce over noodles and sprinkle with Parmesan cheese.

Serves 4

Nutrition Facts

Nutrition (per serving): 148.9 calories; 5% calories from fat; 1.0g total fat; 0.7mg cholesterol; 298.9mg sodium; 460.3mg potassium; 31.0g carbohydrates; 5.5g fiber; 7.3g sugar; 6.2g protein.

Hush Puppy Chicken Casserole

1/2 package corn muffin mix - (8 1/2 oz pkg)
2 tsp chili powder
3 boneless skinless chicken breast halves, cut 1/2" chunks
1 can oven baked beans - (16 oz)
1 can stewed tomatoes - (14 1/2 oz), undrained
1 Tbs smoky-flavored barbecue sauce
2 cups thawed frozen green beans
1/4 tsp dill
1 Tbs maple syrup

Preheat oven to 400 degrees. Prepare half of the corn muffin mix, substituting 1 egg white for the egg and using skim milk in place of whole milk. Set aside.

Sprinkle chili powder onto chicken chunks. Cook chicken over medium heat in a nonstick pan until opaque. Stir in baked beans, stewed tomatoes, and barbecue sauce. Mix frozen green beans with dill. Add to chicken mixture. Simmer 5 to 10 minutes.

Spray a 9- by 13-inch baking dish with nonstick spray. Pour chicken mixture into baking dish. Dot corn muffin batter on top of chicken mixture. Bake for 20 to 25 minutes or until topping is golden. Remove from oven and brush with maple syrup.

Serves 8

Nutrition Facts

Nutrition (per serving): 240.0 calories; 18% calories from fat; 5.0g total fat; 30.0mg cholesterol; 670.0mg sodium; 32.0g carbohydrates; 2.0g fiber; 17.0g protein.

Lamb-Vegetable Kabobs

=== **MARINADE** ===
1/4 cup chopped fresh coriander
1/4 cup chopped fresh mint
1 green chili pepper, seeded, chopped
3 garlic cloves, sliced
2 Tbs grated fresh ginger
1/2 cup nonfat yogurt
1 tsp ground cumin
1 tsp ground coriander
1/2 tsp ground cinnamon
1 pinch ground cloves
12 oz lean lamb from leg, cut into 1" cubes
=== **KABOBS** ===
1 large onion
1 sweet red pepper, cut into 1" cubes
1 yellow pepper, cut into 1" cubes
1 zucchini, cut into 1" cubes
1 yellow squash, cut into 1" cubes
=== **COUSCOUS** ===
2 cups defatted stock
2 cups couscous

To make the marinade: In a food processor grind together the fresh coriander, mint, chili pepper, garlic and ginger (or finely chop by hand). Place in a mixing bowl with the yogurt, cumin, ground coriander, cinnamon and cloves. Add the lamb and mix well. Allow to marinate for at least 2 to 3 hours in the refrigerator.

To make the kabobs: Peel the onion and trim off the root hairs, leaving the root stem attached. Cut into 1-inch wedges, leaving the root on each section so wedges don't separate. Add the onions, red peppers, yellow peppers, zucchini and squash to marinade mixture. Mix to coat well.

Preheat the broiler or light a charcoal or gas grill, allowing it to get very hot. Thread meat and vegetables onto metal or bamboo skewers.

Grill over high heat for 15 to 20 minutes, turning skewers to cook all sides, until meat is cooked as desired.

To make the couscous: While the lamb is cooking, bring the stock to a boil in a 1-quart saucepan. Add the couscous. Cover the pan and remove it from the heat. Let stand for 3 to 4 minutes, or until all the liquid has been absorbed. Fluff with fork. Serve hot with the lamb.

Variations: You may substitute small mushrooms, cherry tomatoes or cubes of eggplant for any of the other vegetables. You may also substitute cubes of lean beef for the lamb. Try cooked bulgur or rice in place of the couscous.

Make-Ahead tip: Prepare the yogurt marinade early in the day or even the night before. Add the lamb and refrigerate until ready to cook.

Comments: Lamb kabobs, marinated in yogurt and a multitude of spices is sure to be a hit at the dinner table. The fresh taste of this dish is enhanced by the use of fresh herbs and vegetables.

Serves 4

Nutrition Facts

Nutrition (per serving): 281.0 calories; 18% calories from fat; 5.7g total fat; 56.0mg cholesterol; 8.6g fiber.

Loose Beef Fajitas

12 oz ground sirloin beef
1 cup chopped onions
1/2 cup chopped green peppers
1/2 cup chopped sweet red peppers
2 garlic cloves, minced
2 tsp chili powder
1/2 tsp ground cumin
1 cup chunky salsa
1/2 cup chopped tomatoes
8 corn or flour tortillas, warmed

In a large nonstick skillet, cook the beef, onions, green and red peppers and garlic over medium heat about 5 minutes or until the beef is browned and the vegetables are tender, stirring frequently. Stir in the chili powder and cumin and cook for 1 minute. Add the salsa and tomatoes. Bring to a gentle boil, then reduce the heat. Simmer, uncovered, for 4 to 5 minutes or until the liquid reduces slightly, stirring occasionally.

To serve, spoon some of the beef mixture just below the center on each of the tortillas. Fold the bottom edge of each tortilla over the filling, then fold in the sides and roll up to enclose the filling.

This recipe yields 4 servings.

Slimming strategy: For an easy, low-fat Mexican topping, stir a small amount of chili powder or cumin, or chopped cucumbers, green onions or your favorite fresh vegetable, into nonfat sour cream or plain yogurt. Or top your entree with salsa; 2 tablespoons of a low-fat brand contains only about 8 calories and no fat.

Comments: Not only is this recipe fast and tasty, it is lower in fat and calories than the traditional fajita recipes.

Serves 4

Nutrition Facts

Nutrition (per serving): 303.0 calories; 25% calories from fat; 8.7g total fat; 52.0mg cholesterol; 5.8g fiber.

Mexican Beef and Cheese Wontons with Salsa

2 servings cooking spray
2 tsp olive oil
1/2 lb lean ground sirloin
2 oz low-fat cheddar or Colby cheese, shredded
2 Tbs chopped green chilies, minced
1 tsp chili powder
1 tsp ground cumin
30 wonton wrappers
1/2 cup salsa

Preheat oven to 350 degrees. Coat a large baking sheet with cooking spray.

Heat oil in a small skillet over medium-high heat. Add beef and cook until meat is browned, breaking up meat as it cooks, about 5 minutes. Drain meat. Add cheese, chilies, chili powder and cumin and cook until cheese melts, stirring frequently, about 1 minute.

Place wonton wrappers on a flat surface. Drop meat mixture by teaspoonfuls onto center of each wrapper. Moisten edges of wrapper with wet fingers, fold over to cover filling, press down firmly to seal and then gently twist ends to form a "firecracker" shape. Transfer filled wrappers to prepared baking sheet and coat surface with cooking spray.

Bake until wontons are golden brown, about 15 minutes. Serve with prepared salsa.

Serves 6

Nutrition Facts

Nutrition (per serving): 587.8 calories; 15% calories from fat; 10.4g total fat; 36.0mg cholesterol; 1153.8mg sodium; 340.1mg potassium; 94.8g carbohydrates; 3.4g fiber; 0.7g sugar; 26.0g protein.

Moo Shu Beef Lettuce Cups

1 serving cooking spray = (5 one-second sprays per serving)
1 lb uncooked lean ground beef (with 7% fat)
1 cup thinly-sliced yellow onion
2 Tbs minced fresh ginger root
2 medium garlic cloves, minced
2 cups thinly-sliced bok choy
1 medium sweet red pepper, thinly sliced
2 cups thinly-sliced button mushrooms -, (abt 10 mushrooms)
2 Tbs low-sodium soy sauce
8 bibb lettuce leaves

Coat a large nonstick skillet with cooking spray and set pan over medium-high heat. Add beef, onion, ginger and garlic; cook until beef is browned and onion is soft, breaking up meat as it cooks, about 5 to 7 minutes.

Add bok choy, pepper, mushrooms and soy sauce; cook until bok choy is wilted and pepper is tender-crisp, about 3 to 5 minutes.

Spoon about 1/2 cup of beef mixture into each lettuce leaf. Serve with extra soy sauce if desired.

Serves 4

Nutrition Facts

Nutrition (per serving): 185.7 calories; 44% calories from fat; 8.9g total fat; 55.3mg cholesterol; 209.4mg sodium; 489.5mg potassium; 7.5g carbohydrates; 1.6g fiber; 3.5g sugar; 18.7g protein.

Orange Beef Stir-Fry

1 1/4 cup reduced-sodium fat-free chicken broth
3 Tbs low-sodium soy sauce
1 tsp Splenda No Calorie Sweetener
1/2 tsp orange extract, (optional)
1 serving cooking spray
2 Tbs freshly-grated orange zest
1/4 cup julienned peeled fresh ginger root
2 medium garlic cloves, slivered
1/4 tsp red pepper flakes, crushed
1 lb lean boneless sirloin beef, trimmed, and
sliced against grain 1/8"-thk strips
4 cups sugar snap peas
1 Tbs arrowroot, dissolved in
1 Tbs water

Whisk broth, soy sauce, Splenda, and orange extract (if using) in a small bowl; set aside.

Coat a large nonstick wok (or skillet) with cooking spray and set over medium-high heat. Add orange peel, ginger and garlic; stir-fry until softened and aromatic, about 2 minutes. Add red pepper flakes and stir-fry 20 seconds.

(NOTE: To julienne means to cut into thin matchsticks. Peel an orange, press the rind sections as flat as you can on a cutting board, and slice them into long matchsticks. For the ginger, cut the peeled stalk into thin, even slices, then cut each of these into matchsticks.)

Add beef; stir-fry until lightly browned, about 2 minutes. Add sugar snap peas and continue stir-frying until crisp-tender, about 2 minutes.

Pour in broth mixture and bring to a simmer. Cover wok (or skillet) and cook 1 minute more.

Stir in arrowroot mixture; cook just until thickened, less than 10 seconds. The moment sauce thickens, remove pan from heat and serve at once.

Serves 4

Nutrition Facts

Nutrition (per serving): 310.8 calories; 47% calories from fat; 16.5g total fat; 59.0mg cholesterol; 686.7mg sodium; 682.0mg potassium; 12.2g carbohydrates; 3.2g fiber; 4.3g sugar; 27.4g protein.

Orange Rosemary Roasted Chicken

3 chicken breast halves
3 chicken legs with thigh pieces
2 garlic cloves
1 1/2 tsp olive oil
3 tsp rosemary
1/3 cup orange juice
Freshly-ground black pepper, to taste

Preheat oven to 450 degrees. Remove skin from chicken. Rub each piece with garlic. Dab fingers in oil and rub each piece with oil. Top with rosemary. Place into a baking dish. Pour in orange juice. Cover and cook for 30 minutes. Turn chicken and return to the oven uncovered for 10 to 15 minutes longer or until "browned." Do not let dry out.

Serves 6

Nutrition Facts

Nutrition (per serving): 165.0 calories; 27% calories from fat; 5.0g total fat; 86.0mg cholesterol; 80.0mg sodium; 28.0g protein.

Roasted and Stuffed Smothered Eggplant

2 medium eggplants, sliced lengthwise
2 tsp olive oil
1 serving cooking spray
1 large onion, chopped 1/4" pieces
1 large carrot, chopped 1/4" pieces
2 medium sweet red peppers, chopped 1/4" pieces
3 large garlic cloves, chopped
3 medium Portobello mushroom caps, chopped 1/2" dice
2 Tbs parsley, fresh, chopped
1 Tbs fresh thyme
1/8 tsp table salt, or to taste
1/8 tsp freshly-ground black pepper, or to taste
15 oz canned tomato sauce

Preheat oven to 400 degrees.

Rub cut sides of eggplants with oil. Place on a nonstick baking sheet cut-sides up. Bake for 20 to 25 minutes (eggplant should not be cooked entirely through). Remove from oven and flip over with a spatula; let cool on baking sheet. Leave oven on.

Meanwhile, coat a large nonstick skillet with cooking spray and heat over medium-high heat. Add onions, carrot and peppers. Sauté until soft and slightly browned, about 5 to 7 minutes. Add garlic and mushrooms. Increase heat to high and continue to sauté until mushrooms soften and release their juices, about 5 to 7 minutes. Remove from heat and stir in parsley and thyme; season to taste with salt and pepper.

Scoop out flesh of cooled eggplant with a soup spoon, leaving about a 1/4-inch of eggplant flesh in skin. Coarsely chop flesh and add to mushroom mixture; mix well.

Fill each eggplant shell with about 1 1/2 cups of filling. Place stuffed eggplant shells in a nonstick 9- by 13-inch pan. Spoon 1/2 cup of tomato sauce over each stuffed eggplant shell. Bake for 15 minutes, remove from oven and let cool.

Freezing and thawing instructions: Freeze each cooled eggplant half, topped with sauce, in individual containers. When ready to eat, thaw and microwave. Or, thaw and reheat for about 15 to 20 minutes in a 350 degrees oven.

Serves 4

Nutrition Facts

Nutrition (per serving): 201.1 calories; 16% calories from fat; 3.8g total fat; 0.0mg cholesterol; 704.0mg sodium; 1860.2mg potassium; 40.9g carbohydrates; 15.6g fiber; 18.5g sugar; 8.7g protein.

Salmon Burgers with Peach Salsa

2 large peaches, diced
1 medium jalapeño pepper, cored, seeded, finely chopped
1 tsp fresh lemon juice
1 1/2 tsp sugar
1/8 tsp table salt
2 Tbs chopped fresh cilantro
14 3/4 oz canned red salmon, drained, and broken into small chunks
1 medium scallion, finely chopped
2 1/2 tsp lemon zest
1 large egg, beaten
1/4 tsp freshly-ground black pepper
3 1/2 Tbs dried bread crumbs, whole-wheat variety

To prepare salsa, combine peaches, jalapeño and lemon juice in a medium bowl; add sugar and mix well. Stir in salt and cilantro and toss gently to mix; set aside.

Preheat grill.

To prepare burgers, mash salmon bones with the back of a fork. Combine salmon, scallion, lemon zest, egg, black pepper and bread crumbs in a medium bowl; mix well. Shape salmon mixture into four 1-inch-thick patties.

Gently place burgers in a grill basket or on a grill rack and grill at medium-high heat for 3 to 5 minutes. Flip burgers and grill until golden brown on both sides, about 3 minutes more. Serve salmon burgers with peach salsa on the side.

Serves 4

Nutrition Facts

Nutrition (per serving): 362.3 calories; 46% calories from fat; 18.6g total fat; 61.3mg cholesterol; 138.7mg sodium; 212.9mg potassium; 14.1g carbohydrates; 1.9g fiber; 8.6g sugar; 35.6g protein.

Savory Beef Burgers

1 lb uncooked lean ground beef (with 7% fat)
2 Tbs minced onion
3/4 tsp Italian seasoning
1/4 tsp ground cumin
1/4 tsp freshly-ground black pepper
1/4 tsp table salt
8 pieces lettuce
1 medium tomato, cut 8 slices
8 slices red onion
1 Tbs Dijon mustard
4 reduced-calorie hamburger rolls

Heat grill or grill pan. Combine beef, onion, mustard, Italian seasoning, cumin, pepper and salt until thoroughly mixed.

Divide beef mixture into 4 equal portions and form patties.

Place patties onto grill or grill pan; cook for 8 to 10 minutes, until desired degree of doneness, turning once.

To assemble, place one patty on one half of each bun. Top each with 2 lettuce leaves, 2 tomato slices, 2 onion slices and other half of bun.

Serves 4

Nutrition Facts

Nutrition (per serving): 284.9 calories; 16% calories from fat; 5.6g total fat; 15.6mg cholesterol; 355.1mg sodium; 3225.0mg potassium; 48.9g carbohydrates; 27.7g fiber; 16.2g sugar; 22.3g protein.

Scallops with Red Pepper Sauce

1 large red bell pepper, cut into fourths
1/8 tsp salt
10 drops red pepper sauce
1 clove garlic, finely chopped
1/4 cup plain nonfat yogurt
1 lb bay scallops
1/4 cup sliced green onions (with tops)
Cilantro leaves

Place steamer basket in 1/2-inch water in saucepan or skillet (water should not touch bottom of basket). Place bell pepper in basket. Cover tightly and heat to boiling; reduce heat. Steam 8 to 10 minutes or until tender. Place bell pepper, salt, pepper sauce and garlic in blender or food processor. Cover and blend on medium speed until almost smooth. Heat in -quart saucepan over medium heat, stirring occasionally, until hot; remove from heat. Gradually stir in yogurt; keep warm. Spray 10-inch nonstick skillet with nonstick cooking spray. Heat over medium-high heat. Add scallops and onions; stir-fry 4 to 5 minutes or until scallops are white in center. Serve sauce with scallops. Garnish with cilantro.

MICROWAVE DIRECTIONS: Prepare bell pepper as directed-- except place in -quart microwavable casserole. Add 1/4 cup water. Cover tightly and microwave on high 4 to 5 minutes, stirring after 2 minutes, until tender; drain. Blend as directed. Pour into 1-quart microwavable casserole. Cover tightly and microwave on high 30 to 60 seconds or until hot. Stir in yogurt. Mix scallops and onions in 1-1/2-quart microwavable casserole. Cover tightly and microwave on high 4 to 6 minutes, stirring every 2 minutes, until scallops are white in center; drain.

Serves 4

Nutrition Facts

Nutrition (per serving): 147.6 calories; 12% calories from fat; 1.9g total fat; 61.0mg cholesterol; 385.7mg sodium; 658.6mg potassium; 3.6g carbohydrates; 0.8g fiber; 1.4g sugar; 27.6g protein.

Thai Stir-Fry Chicken

3 Tbs sesame oil
12 oz skinless, boneless chicken breast, thinly sliced
salt and pepper
8 shallots. sliced
2 garlic cloves, finely chopped
2 tbs grated fresh gingerroot
1 fresh green chili, seeded and finely chopped
1 red bell pepper, seeded and thinly sliced
1 green bell pepper, seeded and thinly sliced
3 zucchini, thinly sliced
2 Tbs ground almonds
1 tsp ground cinnamon
1 Tbs oyster sauce
1/4 oz creamed coconut, grated

Heat the oil in a preheated wok or heavy bottom skillet. Add the chicken and season to taste with salt and pepper, then stir-fry over medium heat for 4 minutes.

Add the shallots, garlic , ginger, and chili and stir-fry for an additional 2 minutes.

Add the red and green bell peppers and zucchini and stir-fry for 1 minute.

Stir in the almonds, cinnamon, oyster sauce, and creamed coconut and season to taste with salt and pepper. Stir- fry for 1 minute to heat through, then serve immediately.

Serves 4

Nutrition Facts

Nutrition (per serving): 184.0 calories; 26% calories from fat; 5.0g total fat; 8.0g carbohydrates; 6.0g sugar; 24.0g protein.

Cooking Tips

Creamed coconut is sold in supermarkets and Asian stores. It is a useful pantry standby because it adds richness and depth of flavor.

Tomato and Tarragon Braised Sole

1 1/4 lbs sole - (four 5-oz fillets)
1/8 tsp table salt, or to taste
1/8 tsp freshly-ground black pepper, or to taste
14 1/2 oz canned diced tomatoes with garlic and onion
1 tsp dried tarragon
2 cups cooked white rice
1 cup chopped green chilies

Coat a large nonstick skillet with cooking spray and set pan over medium-high heat.

Season both sides of sole with salt and pepper; add fillets to pan. Cook until golden, about 1 to 2 minutes per side. Add tomatoes and tarragon and simmer until fish is fork-tender, about 2 minutes. Serve sole and tomato sauce with rice on the side.

Serves 4

Nutrition Facts

Nutrition (per serving): 326.5 calories; 7% calories from fat; 2.8g total fat; 96.4mg cholesterol; 600.7mg sodium; 936.8mg potassium; 35.8g carbohydrates; 2.8g fiber; 1.6g sugar; 38.8g protein.

Turkey Cordon Bleu

1 Tbs all-purpose flour
1/4 tsp freshly-ground black pepper
1/4 tsp poultry seasoning
4 boneless skinless turkey breast cutlets -, (3 oz ea)
1 Tbs olive oil
1 cup thinly-sliced mushrooms
1 onion, chopped
1/4 cup chopped lean ham
2 slices part-skim mozzarella cheese - (3/4 oz ea), halved
1/4 cup canned pimientos, julienned

Preheat the oven to 350 degrees. Spray an 8-inch square baking pan with nonstick cooking spray.

In a gallon-size sealable plastic bag, combine the flour, pepper and poultry seasoning. Add the turkey; shake to coat.

In a large nonstick skillet, heat the oil. Add the turkey and cook until lightly browned, about 2 minutes on each side. Transfer to the baking pan.

In the same skillet, combine the mushrooms, onion and ham; cook, stirring constantly, until softened, about 5 minutes. Spoon evenly over the turkey; top each cutlet with a cheese slice. Bake until the turkey is cooked through, about 15 minutes. Serve garnished with the pimiento strips.

Serves 4

Nutrition Facts

Nutrition (per serving): 186.0 calories; 30% calories from fat; 6.0g total fat; 63.0mg cholesterol; 180.0mg sodium; 5.0g carbohydrates; 1.0g fiber; 26.0g protein.

Side Dishes & Vegetables

Asparagus with Hazelnut Butter
Baby Minted Carrots
Black-Eyed Peas, Creole Style
Broccoli Rabe with Pine Nuts
Brown Rice Pilaf with Asparagus and Mushrooms
Chili-Lime Corn
Chinese-Style Asparagus
Couscous with Mushrooms and Curry
'Fried' Onion Rings
Fruited Basmati Rice
Garlic Mashed Potatoes
Green Rice
Hash Browns
Japanese Grilled Eggplant
Leeks au Gratin
Lemon-Ginger Asparagus
Mixed Rice Pilaf
New Potatoes with Parmesan and Sage
Roasted Chickpeas
Saucy Jerusalem Artichokes
Slow Cooker Red Beans and Rice
String beans In Walnut Sauce
Wild Rice Pilaf

Asparagus with Hazelnut Butter

1 lb fresh asparagus
2 Tbs butter
1 Tbs chopped hazelnuts

Steam asparagus until tender. Place into a serving dish. In a sauté pan melt the butter; add hazelnuts. Sauté until butter turns golden brown - - do not let butter burn. Pour over asparagus and serve.

Serves 4

Nutrition Facts

Nutrition (per serving): 95.0 calories; 66% calories from fat; 7.0g total fat; 15.0mg cholesterol; 60.0mg sodium; 5.0g carbohydrates; 1.5g fiber; 3.0g protein.

Baby Minted Carrots

1 lb baby carrots
6 cups water
1/4 cup apple juice
1 Tbs cornstarch
1/2 Tbs chopped fresh mint leaves
1 dash cinnamon

Scrub carrots. Put 6 cups of water into a large pan. Boil carrots until tender crisp; about 10 minutes. Over moderate heat, thicken apple juice with cornstarch. Add mint and cinnamon. Pour over carrots.

This recipe yields 5 servings.

Serves 5

Nutrition Facts

Nutrition (per serving): 50.0 calories; 0% calories from fat; 0.0g total fat; 30.0mg sodium; 12.0g carbohydrates; 3.0g fiber; 1.0g protein.

Black-Eyed Peas, Creole Style

2 cups black-eyed peas
3 cups water
1 chicken-flavored bouillon cube
2 cups canned tomatoes, crushed
1 large onion, finely chopped
2 celery stalks, finely chopped
3 tsp minced garlic
1/2 tsp dry mustard
1/4 tsp ground ginger
1/4 tsp cayenne pepper
1 bay leaf
1/2 cup chopped parsley for garnish

Place black-eyed peas in a medium saucepan. Cover with 2 cups of water, bring to boil for 2 minutes, cover, remove from heat and let stand for 1 hour. Drain the soaking liquid.

Add the remaining 1 cup of water, bouillon cube, tomatoes and juice, chopped onion, chopped celery, garlic, mustard, ginger, cayenne pepper and bay leaf. Stir together, bring to a boil, cover again, reduce heat and simmer slowly for 2 hours. Stir occasionally and add water to keep the peas covered with liquid.

Remove the bay leaf, pour into a serving bowl and garnish with parsley. (Raw, chopped onion also may be used.)

Serves 8

Nutrition Facts

Nutrition (per serving): 142.0 calories; 12% calories from fat; 2.0g total fat; 1.0mg cholesterol; 705.0mg sodium; 23.0g carbohydrates; 7.0g fiber; 8.0g protein.

Broccoli Rabe with Pine Nuts

6 cups broccoli rabe, rinsed, and large stems removed - (abt 2 bunches)
2 tsp olive oil
2 medium garlic cloves, minced
1/8 tsp freshly-ground black pepper, or to taste
1/8 tsp table salt, or to taste
2 Tbs pine nuts, toasted

Blanch broccoli rabe in a large pot of boiling water for 2 minutes; drain.

In a large skillet, heat oil. Add garlic and cook 1 minute. Add broccoli rabe and cook 4 minutes; season with salt and pepper.

Add pine nuts, toss and serve.

Serves 4

Nutrition Facts

Nutrition (per serving): 62.2 calories; 74% calories from fat; 5.4g total fat; 0.0mg cholesterol; 89.6mg sodium; 130.6mg potassium; 2.5g carbohydrates; 1.6g fiber; 0.3g sugar; 2.3g protein.

Brown Rice Pilaf with Asparagus and Mushrooms

1 Tbs margarine
1 small onion, chopped
1/2 lb fresh mushrooms, thinly sliced
1 cup brown rice
3 cups water
1 chicken-flavored bouillon cube
1/2 lb asparagus
1/8 tsp nutmeg
2 Tbs finely-grated Swiss cheese
1/2 cup chopped parsley, for garnish

In a saucepan heat the margarine and sauté the onions and mushrooms over medium heat until softened. Add the rice and stir. Add the water, bouillon cube and nutmeg. Bring mixture to a boil, reduce heat, cover and simmer for 35 minutes.

Cut asparagus into 1-inch pieces (discard woody stems). Stir asparagus into the rice mixture, cover, and cook another 5 minutes. Stir in the grated cheese and garnish generously with parsley.

Serves 6

Nutrition Facts

Nutrition (per serving): 230.0 calories; 27% calories from fat; 7.0g total fat; 10.0mg cholesterol; 840.0mg sodium; 30.0g carbohydrates; 3.0g fiber; 12.0g protein.

Chili-Lime Corn

1 tsp chili powder
1 tsp lime zest
1 1/2 Tbs fresh lime juice
1 tsp table salt
4 pieces corn on the cob

Preheat grill. Stir together chili powder, lime zest and juice, and salt; brush over husked corn.
Grill corn over medium heat until tender and lightly charred, about 10 minutes.

Serves 4

Nutrition Facts

Nutrition (per serving): 136.6 calories; 7% calories from fat; 1.2g total fat; 0.0mg cholesterol; 989.9mg sodium; 402.2mg potassium; 32.6g carbohydrates; 4.2g fiber; 5.2g sugar; 4.3g protein.

Chinese-Style Asparagus

1 1/2 lbs fresh asparagus
1 tsp soy sauce
1/2 tsp sugar
1/2 cup water

Cut asparagus into 1 1/2-inch lengths. Boil water, soy sauce and sugar in a large sauté pan over high heat. Add asparagus and reduce heat to low. Simmer until tender-crisp (about 5 minutes). Serve.

Serves 6

Nutrition Facts

Nutrition (per serving): 32.0 calories; 0% calories from fat; 0.0g total fat; 0.0mg cholesterol; 60.0mg sodium; 5.0g carbohydrates; 1.5g fiber; 3.0g protein.

Couscous with Mushrooms and Curry

1/2 cup sliced onion
2 tsp minced garlic
1 tsp olive oil
1 cup sliced mushrooms
1/2 cup grated carrots
1 tsp curry powder
1/4 tsp turmeric
1/2 tsp ground coriander
2 tsp cinnamon
1/2 cup raisins
3 cups defatted Chicken Stock
2 Tbs low-sodium soy or tamari sauce
1/2 cup chopped parsley
2 cups uncooked couscous

In a large skillet over medium-high heat, sauté onions and garlic in oil for 2 minutes, stirring frequently. Add mushrooms and carrots and cook for 5 minutes.

Add curry powder, turmeric, coriander, cinnamon, and raisins, and cook for 3 minutes more. Add stock and bring to a boil.

Stir in soy sauce, parsley, and couscous. Cover pan and remove from heat. Let it sit for 15 minutes. Fluff couscous with a fork. Serve hot.

Serves 4

Nutrition Facts

Nutrition (per serving): 495.8 calories; 7% calories from fat; 4.3g total fat; 5.4mg cholesterol; 585.8mg sodium; 705.2mg potassium; 96.9g carbohydrates; 7.3g fiber; 17.2g sugar; 18.0g protein.

'Fried' Onion Rings

3 servings olive oil cooking spray
1/4 cup all-purpose flour
1/4 tsp garlic powder
1/8 tsp dry mustard
1/4 tsp table salt
2 large Spanish onions, sliced 1/4"-thk rounds,
and separated into rings
1/2 cup buttermilk
1 cup seasoned bread crumbs

Preheat oven to 400 degrees. Coat a large baking sheet with cooking spray.

In a large bowl, combine flour, garlic powder, dry mustard and salt. Add onions and toss to coat.

Pour buttermilk into another large bowl, add onions and toss to coat (use your hands for the best result).

Place bread crumbs in another large bowl, add onions and toss to coat. Transfer onions to prepared baking sheet and spray with cooking spray.

Bake until golden brown, about 35 minutes. Serve hot.

Serves 4

Nutrition Facts

Nutrition (per serving): 233.1 calories; 16% calories from fat; 4.3g total fat; 0.3mg cholesterol; 529.2mg sodium; 194.7mg potassium; 42.1g carbohydrates; 2.8g fiber; 6.6g sugar; 6.3g protein.

Fruited Basmati Rice

2 1/2 cups uncooked basmati rice
1 Tbs olive oil
1/2 orange
5 slices ginger root, chopped
1/4 cup golden raisins
1/2 cup dried apricots, chopped
1/2 tsp cumin seed
1/4 cup slivered almonds

Place the rice into a pan and rinse it with water to remove milky coating (until water runs clear). Bring to a boil in ample water. Reduce heat to very low, cover the pan and simmer.

Grate the peel from 1/2 and orange. Add to the simmering rice. Peel the ginger root, cut 5 slices, chop and stir them into the rice. Add the raisins and dried chopped apricots. Sprinkle the rice mixture with cumin. Cover and cook for a total of 30 minutes.

Just before serving, toast the almonds in a heavy sauté pan until fragrant and light brown. Top each serving of rice with toasted almonds.

Serves 8

Nutrition Facts

Nutrition (per serving): 285.0 calories; 12% calories from fat; 4.0g total fat; 0.0mg cholesterol; 5.0mg sodium; 57.0g carbohydrates; 2.5g fiber; 5.0g protein.

Garlic Mashed Potatoes

6 large peeled Yukon Gold or Idaho potatoes
(approximately six cups)
10 garlic cloves
1 bay leaf
1 tsp salt
1/4 cup buttermilk - (to 1 cup)
Salt, to taste
Freshly-ground black pepper, to taste

In a large pot, combine the potatoes, garlic cloves, bay leaf and salt with just enough water to cover. Cover the pot, bring to a boil, then lower the heat and simmer for 15 to 20 minutes, or until the potatoes are tender. Drain. Discard the bay leaf.

Using a potato masher; mash the potatoes and garlic with enough buttermilk to achieve a smooth consistency. Add salt and pepper to taste.

Serves 6

Nutrition Facts

Nutrition (per serving): 170.0 calories; 21% calories from fat; 4.0g total fat; 1.0mg cholesterol; 170.0mg sodium.

Green Rice

1/2 cup minced green onion
2 Tbs minced garlic
1 tsp olive oil
1/4 cup dry sherry or white wine
1/2 cup chopped parsley
1/3 cup minced spinach leaves
2 Tbs minced fresh basil
3 cups cooked long-grain brown rice
2 Tbs pine nuts
2 Tbs red bell pepper, minced
1/4 cup grated Parmesan cheese

In a large skillet over medium-high heat, sauté green onion and garlic in olive oil and sherry for 5 minutes, stirring frequently. Add parsley, spinach, and basil and cook for 3 more minutes.

Add rice and pine nuts and heat through, stirring constantly, for about minutes. Remove from heat and stir in bell pepper and Parmesan cheese. Serve hot.

Serves 4

Nutrition Facts

Nutrition (per serving): 265.5 calories; 23% calories from fat; 7.3g total fat; 5.5mg cholesterol; 113.1mg sodium; 236.5mg potassium; 39.1g carbohydrates; 3.7g fiber; 1.3g sugar; 7.7g protein.

Hash Browns

2 large Idaho potatoes, peeled, shredded
2 tsp olive oil
1/2 tsp paprika
1/2 tsp table salt
1/4 tsp freshly-ground black pepper
1/3 cup reduced-sodium chicken broth
2 Tbs red wine vinegar

Place potatoes in a large saucepan and add enough water to cover. Set pan over medium-high heat and bring to a boil. Boil 5 minutes. Drain and set aside.

Heat oil in a large, nonstick skillet over medium-high heat. Add potatoes, paprika, salt and pepper; stir to coat. Sauté 2 minutes. Add chicken broth and vinegar and cook until liquid is absorbed, stirring frequently, about 3 minutes.

Serves 4

Nutrition Facts

Nutrition (per serving): 70.6 calories; 29% calories from fat; 2.4g total fat; 0.0mg cholesterol; 335.1mg sodium; 349.6mg potassium; 11.7g carbohydrates; 1.1g fiber; 0.0g sugar; 1.4g protein.

Japanese Grilled Eggplant

4 medium Japanese eggplants - (abt 1 lb), sliced crosswise on the diagonal into 1/2"-thk pieces
1 serving cooking spray = (5 one-second sprays per serving)
2 Tbs low-sodium soy sauce
1 Tbs fresh lemon juice
1 1/2 tsp rice wine vinegar
1 tsp freshly-grated ginger root
1/4 tsp minced garlic
1/4 cup thinly-sliced scallions, sliced on diagonal

Preheat outdoor grill, stove-top grill pan or broiler. Coat eggplant with cooking spray. (Note: If you can't find any Japanese eggplants, buy regular eggplants that are small in size.)

Grill or broil eggplant turning as needed until lightly charred and tender, about 7 to 9 minutes.

Whisk soy sauce, lemon juice, vinegar, ginger and garlic in a small bowl until blended. Drizzle over grilled eggplant and sprinkle with scallions.

Serves 4

Nutrition Facts

Nutrition (per serving): 17.1 calories; 10% calories from fat; 0.2g total fat; 0.0mg cholesterol; 301.8mg sodium; 120.2mg potassium; 4.1g carbohydrates; 1.2g fiber; 1.1g sugar; 0.9g protein.

Leeks au Gratin

4 medium leeks with tops (about 2 pounds),
cut into 1/2-inch pieces
Crumb Topping
1 Tbs margarine
1 Tbs plus
1 tsp all-purpose flour
1/4 tsp salt
1 dash pepper
2/3 cup skim milk
1/2 cup shredded Gruyere cheese (2 ounces)
CRUMB TOPPING
2 Tbs dry bread crumbs
1 tsp margarine, melted

Heat 1 inch water to boiling. Add leeks. Cover and cook over medium heat about 5 minutes or until crisp-tender; drain. Heat oven to 325 degrees. Prepare Crumb Topping. Spray shallow 1-quart casserole with nonstick cooking spray. Heat margarine in 2-quart saucepan over low heat. Stir in flour, salt and pepper. Cook over low heat, stirring constantly, until margarine is absorbed; remove from heat. Gradually stir in milk. Heat to boiling, stirring constantly. Boil and stir 1 minute. Stir in cheese until melted. Stir in leeks. Pour into casserole. Sprinkle with Crumb Topping. Bake uncovered about 25 minutes or until heated through.
CRUMB TOPPING Mix all ingredients.

Serves 4

Nutrition Facts

Nutrition (per serving): 207.7 calories; 51% calories from fat; 12.0g total fat; 23.2mg cholesterol; 329.0mg sodium; 249.1mg potassium; 17.7g carbohydrates; 1.8g fiber; 5.8g sugar; 8.2g protein.

Lemon-Ginger Asparagus

1 1/2 lbs asparagus, tough ends snapped off
2 Tbs fat-free chicken broth, use a highly-
flavored broth if possible
1/2 tsp freshly-grated ginger root
1 tsp fresh lemon juice
1 Tbs minced scallions
1/4 tsp table salt
1/4 tsp freshly-ground black pepper

Bring 1 to 2 inches of water to a boil in a medium skillet. Place asparagus in skillet, reduce heat to medium and cook until asparagus are crisp-tender, about 6 to 8 minutes; drain well.

Place asparagus in a large glass bowl. Combine broth, ginger, lemon juice, scallion, salt and pepper together in a cup; pour over asparagus. Set aside for 30 minutes to marinate.

Serves 4

Nutrition Facts

Nutrition (per serving): 35.5 calories; 5% calories from fat; 0.2g total fat; 0.0mg cholesterol; 164.4mg sodium; 353.2mg potassium; 7.0g carbohydrates; 3.7g fiber; 3.3g sugar; 3.8g protein.

Mixed Rice Pilaf

1 cup chopped onion
2 tsp minced garlic
1/3 cup minced red bell pepper
1/2 cup minced celery
1/2 cup dry sherry or white wine
2 cups long-grain brown rice
1/2 cup wild rice
1/2 cup basmati rice
4 cups defatted chicken stock
1/2 tsp dried thyme
1/4 tsp dried sage
1 Tbs low-sodium soy or tamari sauce

In a heavy pot over medium-high heat, sauté onion, garlic, red bell pepper, and celery in sherry until vegetables are soft (5 to 10 minutes).

Add brown, wild, and basmati rice. Cook, stirring, for 3 minutes. Add stock, thyme, and sage, and bring to a boil. Lower heat to medium and cook, uncovered, for 15 minutes.

Lower heat to low, cover pot, and let pilaf steam until rice is tender (about 25 minutes). Stir in soy sauce.

Serves 6

Nutrition Facts

Nutrition (per serving): 204.8 calories; 11% calories from fat; 2.7g total fat; 4.8mg cholesterol; 243.0mg sodium; 318.7mg potassium; 32.7g carbohydrates; 2.2g fiber; 4.5g sugar; 7.1g protein.

New Potatoes with Parmesan and Sage

24 small new potatoes
1/2 tsp sage
1/4 cup freshly-grated Parmesan cheese

Place potatoes into a steamer. Sprinkle them with sage and steam until tender. Place into a serving bowl and toss with freshly grated Parmesan cheese.

Serves 6

Nutrition Facts

Nutrition (per serving): 250.0 calories; 7% calories from fat; 2.0g total fat; 3.0mg cholesterol; 95.0mg sodium; 51.0g carbohydrates; 4.0g fiber; 6.0g protein.

Roasted Chickpeas

1 serving olive oil cooking spray = (5 one-second sprays per serving)
2 cups canned chickpeas, drained, rinsed
1/4 tsp garlic powder
1/8 tsp red pepper flakes

Preheat oven to 350 degrees. Lightly coat a rimmed baking sheet with cooking spray.

Spread chickpeas on baking sheet and sprinkle with garlic powder and red pepper; toss to coat.

Roast on bottom rack of oven, shaking pan about every 15 minutes, until browned and slightly crunchy, about 45 to 50 minutes. (The chickpeas will still be somewhat soft. Cook longer for desired texture.) Cool before serving.

Serves 4

Nutrition Facts

Nutrition (per serving): 145.2 calories; 8% calories from fat; 1.5g total fat; 0.0mg cholesterol; 358.9mg sodium; 209.5mg potassium; 27.3g carbohydrates; 5.3g fiber; 0.0g sugar; 6.0g protein.

Saucy Jerusalem Artichokes

1 lb Jerusalem artichokes, cut into 1/4-inch
slices (about 3-1/2 cups)
1 cup skim milk
1 Tbs cornstarch
1 Tbs chopped fresh or
1 tsp freeze-dried chives
1 tsp chopped fresh or
1/2 tsp dried dill weed
1/4 tsp salt
1/8 tsp pepper
3 oz part-skim Swiss cheese shredded (3/4 cup)

Place steamer basket in 1/2-inch water (water should not touch bottom of basket). Place artichokes in basket. Cover tightly and heat to boiling; reduce heat. Steam 10 to 12 minutes or until crisp-tender. Mix remaining ingredients except cheese in 2-quart saucepan. Cook over medium heat, stirring constantly, until mixture thickens and boils. Boil and stir 1 minute; remove from heat. Stir in cheese until melted. Stir in artichokes.

MICROWAVE DIRECTIONS: Place artichokes and 1/4 cup water in 1-1/2-quart microwavable casserole. Cover tightly and microwave on high 6 to 7 minutes, stirring after 3 minutes, until crisp-tender; drain. Mix remaining ingredients except cheese in 4-cup microwavable measure. Microwave uncovered on high 3 to 4 minutes, stirring every minute, until thickened. Stir in cheese until melted. Stir into artichokes.

Serves 4

Nutrition Facts

Nutrition (per serving): 152.8 calories; 6% calories from fat; 1.1g total fat; 8.6mg cholesterol; 230.7mg sodium; 610.9mg potassium; 25.5g carbohydrates; 1.9g fiber; 14.3g sugar; 10.3g protein.

Slow Cooker Red Beans and Rice

1 serving garlic-flavored cooking spray = (5 one-second sprays per serving)
1 small onion, chopped
1 medium garlic clove, minced
1/2 cup uncooked white rice, converted-variety
1 1/2 cup fat-free chicken broth
14 1/2 oz canned tomato puree, roasted-variety
15 oz canned kidney beans, drained, rinsed
2 slices reduced-fat cooked crisp bacon, crumbled
2 Tbs Spice Islands Chipotle Sauce, or other brand
1/2 tsp dried oregano
1/2 tsp table salt
1/4 tsp freshly-ground black pepper
1 Tbs chopped fresh cilantro
1 Tbs chopped scallions (green part only)

Coat a large nonstick skillet with cooking spray; heat over medium-high heat. Add onion and garlic to skillet and sauté until slightly softened, about 2 to 3 minutes.

Meanwhile, place rice, broth, tomato puree, beans, bacon, chipotle sauce, oregano, salt and pepper in a 3- to 4-quart slow cooker; add sautéed vegetables. Cover and cook on low setting for 3 1/2 hours; stir in cilantro and scallion just before serving.

Serves 4

Nutrition Facts

Nutrition (per serving): 334.0 calories; 6% calories from fat; 2.4g total fat; 10.3mg cholesterol; 884.3mg sodium; 1430.8mg potassium; 65.2g carbohydrates; 14.9g fiber; 11.7g sugar; 17.0g protein.

String Beans in Walnut Sauce

1 lb Fresh string beans
1/4 lb Shelled walnuts
1/4 cup Red wine vinegar
1/4 cup Onion minced
1 cup Chicken stock
2 each Garlic cloves minced
2 tsp Sweet paprika
3 Tbs Cilantro freshly &, finely chopped
1 1/2 tsp Salt
3 quarts Water

In mill or with a mortar & pestle, pulverize the walnuts into a paste. Combine the stock, onions, garlic, paprika, vinegar, salt, walnut paste, & cilantro. Mix thoroughly. Trim but do not cut the string beans. Bring the water to boil, add the string beans and boil them for 10 minutes. Drain the beans well. Add the beans to the walnut paste mixture and toss until coated completely with the mixture. Serve at once.

Serves 6

Nutrition Facts

Nutrition (per serving): 171.2 calories; 63% calories from fat; 13.1g total fat; 1.2mg cholesterol; 652.7mg sodium; 318.3mg potassium; 11.8g carbohydrates; 3.8g fiber; 1.5g sugar; 5.5g protein.

Wild Rice Pilaf

5 cups uncooked wild rice
5 cups boiling water
1 cup chopped onion
2 tsp olive oil
3/4 cup orzo
5 cups defatted Chicken Stock
1/2 cup toasted pine nuts
1/2 cup raisins
herbal salt substitute, to taste

Place rice in a large bowl and cover with the boiling water. Let stand for 10 minutes.

In a large, heavy pot over medium-high heat, sauté onion in olive oil until soft but not browned (about 5 minutes). Add orzo and continue to cook for 2 minutes.

Drain rice from soaking water. Add rice to sautéed onion and orzo and stir constantly until rice sizzles (about 10 minutes).

Pour in stock. Bring to a boil, then lower heat to medium and simmer, covered, until liquid is absorbed (about 45 minutes).

Add toasted pine nuts, raisins, and salt substitute, to taste. Remove from heat, cover, and let stand until raisins soften (about 5 minutes). Serve hot.

Serves 12

Nutrition Facts

Nutrition (per serving): 214.6 calories; 25% calories from fat; 6.2g total fat; 3.0mg cholesterol; 149.1mg sodium; 295.3mg potassium; 33.5g carbohydrates; 2.1g fiber; 6.9g sugar; 7.7g protein.

Soups & Salads

Balsamic Asparagus and Cherry Tomato Salad
Broccoli Soup
Cajun Chicken Salad
Classic Caesar Salad
Classic Midwestern Macaroni Salad
Cream of Broccoli-Cheese Soup
Cream of Zucchini Soup
Cucumber Pineapple Salad
Curried Prawn and Pasta Salad
Eggplant, Tomato and Caper Salad
French Onion Soup
Fresh Corn and Goat Cheese Salad
Fresh Cream of Tomato Soup with Basil
Fresh Curried Corn Soup
Garden Salad with Creamy Herb Dressing
Harvest Chicken Chowder
Hearty Chicken Vegetable Soup
Herbed Split Pea Soup
Home Made French Dressing
Jicama Salad
Lettuce Soup
Manhattan Fish Chowder
Mediterranean Bean Salad
Pumpkin Soup
Saffron Carrot Soup
Southwestern Egg Salad
Tomato, Avocado and Golden Beet Salad
Tomato-Tofu Bisque
Tortellini Soup
Tropical Avocado and Fruit Salad with Creamy Lime Dressing
Zesty Tomato Salad

Balsamic Asparagus and Cherry Tomato Salad

1 1/2 lbs asparagus - (abt 40 spears)
1 cup cherry tomatoes - (abt 10), cut in half
1 Tbs balsamic vinegar
2 tsp orange juice
1 tsp minced garlic
2 Tbs shredded Parmesan cheese
1/8 tsp table salt, or to taste
1/8 tsp freshly-ground black pepper, or to taste

Chop woody ends off asparagus. Microwave for 2 to 3 minutes, or cook in boiling, salted water until barely tender, about 4 to 6 minutes.
Plunge into ice water to stop cooking. Drain. Add cherry tomatoes.
Stir together vinegar, orange juice and garlic; season to taste. Spoon dressing over asparagus and tomatoes.
Sprinkle with Parmesan cheese.

Serves 4

Nutrition Facts

Nutrition (per serving): 55.9 calories; 15% calories from fat; 1.0g total fat; 2.2mg cholesterol; 118.1mg sodium; 446.0mg potassium; 9.3g carbohydrates; 4.0g fiber; 3.4g sugar; 5.1g protein.

Broccoli Soup

1/2 cup chopped onion
1 Tbs margarine
1 Tbs flour
1/2 can chicken broth - (5 oz)
1/2 can water - (5 oz)
10 oz frozen chopped broccoli
1/2 tsp tarragon
1/4 tsp garlic powder
1/4 tsp thyme
Freshly-ground black pepper, to taste
1 cup skim milk

Sauté onion in margarine until soft. Add flour and cook for one minute, stirring constantly. Add chicken broth and water gradually and stir until well-blended. Add broccoli and seasonings. Bring to a boil. Reduce heat, cover and cook until broccoli is tender (about 15 minutes). Add milk and simmer another 5 minutes.

Serves 4

Nutrition Facts

Nutrition (per serving): 100.0 calories; 36% calories from fat; 4.0g total fat; 1.0mg cholesterol; 317.0mg sodium; 10.0g carbohydrates; 0.5g fiber; 6.0g protein.

Cajun Chicken Salad

4 cups lettuce, mixed, leaves
1 cup snow peas, trimmed
12 medium cherry tomatoes
1 cup pear-shaped yellow tomatoes
3/4 cup sliced celery
1/4 cup chopped shallots
1/8 tsp Cajun seasoning, or to taste
10 oz uncooked boneless skinless chicken
breasts
2 Tbs diet Italian salad dressing

Place lettuce in a serving dish and top with vegetables; set aside.
Sprinkle Cajun seasoning over chicken and broil, grill or barbecue it
until cooked. Slice chicken into thin strips.
Arrange warm chicken over salad and drizzle with dressing.

Serves 4

Nutrition Facts

Nutrition (per serving): 131.7 calories; 12% calories from fat; 1.9g
total fat; 41.6mg cholesterol; 86.5mg sodium; 669.8mg potassium;
10.3g carbohydrates; 3.2g fiber; 3.4g sugar; 19.0g protein.

Classic Caesar Salad

1/4 cup fresh lemon juice
2 Tbs water
2 Tbs grated Parmesan cheese
2 medium garlic cloves, sliced
1 tsp olive oil
1 Tbs red wine vinegar
2 average anchovies canned in oil, drained,
and finely chopped or mashed with a fork
1 tsp Dijon mustard
1/2 tsp Worcestershire sauce
1/4 tsp freshly-ground black pepper
4 cup romaine lettuce, chopped, rinsed well and
patted dry sherry

Combine all ingredients, except lettuce, in a blender or food processor; purée until blended. (Note: Omit the anchovies if you do not like their flavor.)
Place lettuce leaves in a large bowl and toss with dressing until well coated.

Serves 2

Nutrition Facts

Nutrition (per serving): 85.8 calories; 45% calories from fat; 4.5g total fat; 7.8mg cholesterol; 277.2mg sodium; 382.5mg potassium; 8.6g carbohydrates; 2.7g fiber; 2.2g sugar; 5.0g protein.

Classic Midwestern Macaroni Salad

2 cups dry whole-wheat elbow macaroni
1 medium celery stalk, diced
1 small sweet red pepper, chopped
1/2 cup cooked frozen peas and carrots
3 medium scallions, chopped
1/2 cup Kraft Free Shredded Cheddar Cheese,
or other brand
1/2 cup fat-free mayonnaise
1/4 cup fat-free sour cream
1/4 cup sliced dill pickles
1/4 tsp onion powder

Cook pasta according to package directions. Drain and rinse with cold water; drain again. Combine cooked pasta, celery, pepper, peas and carrots, scallion and cheese in a large mixing bowl.

To make dressing, combine mayonnaise, sour cream, pickle and onion powder in a small bowl. Pour dressing over pasta mixture and toss lightly to coat. Cover and chill for at least 2 hours.

Serves 12

Nutrition Facts

Nutrition (per serving): 69.3 calories; 13% calories from fat; 1.1g total fat; 2.1mg cholesterol; 260.2mg sodium; 226.4mg potassium; 12.5g carbohydrates; 2.4g fiber; 3.5g sugar; 3.4g protein.

Cream of Broccoli-Cheese Soup

1 onion, chopped
4 cups chopped broccoli
3 small all-purpose potatoes, peeled and cubed
4 cups skim milk
3 packets low-sodium instant chicken broth and seasoning mix
1 carrot, shredded
3/4 cup shredded reduced fat sharp cheddar cheese
1/4 tsp dried sage
1/4 tsp freshly-ground black pepper

Spray a large nonstick saucepan or Dutch oven with nonstick cooking spray; heat. Add the onion and cook, stirring constantly, until softened, about 5 minutes. Add the broccoli, potatoes and 2 cups water; bring to a boil. Reduce the heat and simmer, covered, until the vegetables are tender, about 20 minutes.

With a slotted spoon, transfer the vegetables to a blender or food processor. Puree, then return them to the liquid. Add the milk, broth mix and carrot; bring to a boil. Reduce the heat and simmer, stirring as needed, until the carrot is softened, about 5 minutes.

Remove the pan from the heat; cool about 1 minute. Add the cheese, sage and pepper; stir until the cheese is melted.

Serves 4

Nutrition Facts

Nutrition (per serving): 278.0 calories; 15% calories from fat; 5.0g total fat; 20.0mg cholesterol; 335.0mg sodium; 40.0g carbohydrates; 5.0g fiber; 20.0g protein.

Cream of Zucchini Soup

1 cup minced onion
1/4 cup chopped green onions
2 tsp dark sesame oil
1/4 cup dry sherry
1/4 cup chopped parsley
1 cup chopped zucchini
1/4 cup chopped celery
4 cups defatted Chicken Stock
1/3 cup rolled oats
1 tsp salt, or to taste
1/4 tsp dried thyme
1/4 tsp white pepper
2 tsp chopped fresh dill

In a large pot over medium-high heat, sauté onion and green onion in sesame oil and sherry for 5 minutes, stirring frequently. Add parsley, zucchini, and celery, and cook 10 minutes, stirring occasionally.

Pour in stock, and add oats, salt, thyme, white pepper, and dill. Bring soup to a boil, then lower heat to medium and simmer, covered, for 20 minutes.

Transfer soup to a blender in small amounts and puree until thick and smooth. Return to pot. Taste for seasoning, reheat, and serve.

Serves 6

Nutrition Facts

Nutrition (per serving): 112.1 calories; 28% calories from fat; 3.7g total fat; 4.8mg cholesterol; 640.9mg sodium; 323.1mg potassium; 12.5g carbohydrates; 1.1g fiber; 4.7g sugar; 5.0g protein.

Cucumber Pineapple Salad

1/4 cup sugar
2/3 cup rice wine vinegar
2 Tbs water
1/4 tsp salt
1 cup peeled cored diced fresh pineapple in 1/3
1 cucumber, peeled, sliced thin
1 carrot, peeled, julienned
1/3 cup thinly-sliced red onion
4 cups torn salad greens
1 Tbs toasted sesame seeds

Bring sugar, rice wine vinegar and water to a boil in a heavy saucepan. Stir constantly until reduced to about 1/2 cup -- about 5 minutes.

Transfer to a large bowl and place into refrigerator. When chilled, add pineapple pieces. Cover and return to refrigerator for one hour.

Add cucumber, carrot and red onion to the pineapple mixture. Mix well. Place salad greens onto plates. Top with pineapple mixture. Sprinkle with toasted sesame seeds. Serve.

Serves 4

Nutrition Facts

Nutrition (per serving): 117.0 calories; 7% calories from fat; 1.0g total fat; 0.0mg cholesterol; 150.0mg sodium; 25.0g carbohydrates; 3.0g fiber; 2.0g protein.

Curried Prawn and Pasta Salad

1 lb medium prawns, peeled & deveined
2/3 cup white wine
2 cups rotelle pasta
1/4 tsp pepper
1/2 cup minced celery
1/2 cup low-calorie mayonnaise
1 tsp lemon juice
2 tsp curry powder
lettuce leaves, for decoration
1 Tbs chopped, toasted almonds

In a small saucepan over medium-high heat, place prawns and wine, and cook until prawns turn pink (about 2 minutes). Remove prawns and cut in half. Discard wine.

Cook pasta until al dente (about 8 minutes). Drain and refresh under cold water. In a large bowl mix pasta with cooked prawns, pepper, celery, mayonnaise, lemon juice, and curry powder. Chill 20 minutes. Arrange on a bed of lettuce and garnish with almonds.

Serves 4

Nutrition Facts

Nutrition (per serving): 386.5 calories; 25% calories from fat; 11.2g total fat; 217.3mg cholesterol; 396.7mg sodium; 369.4mg potassium; 35.3g carbohydrates; 1.9g fiber; 0.4g sugar; 28.3g protein.

Eggplant, Tomato and Caper Salad

1 lb eggplant, unpeeled, diced
2 tsp table salt
1 serving cooking spray = (5 one-second
sprays per serving)
1 medium onion, diced
2 medium garlic cloves, minced
1 Tbs sugar
2 medium ripe tomatoes, seeded, diced
3 Tbs sherry-flavored vinegar
3 Tbs capers, chopped if large
2 Tbs chopped fresh parsley
1/8 tsp table salt, or to taste
1/8 tsp freshly-ground black pepper, or to taste

Place eggplant in a colander and sprinkle with 2 teaspoons of salt. Toss and set aside for 10 minutes; rinse and drain.

Spray a large nonstick skillet with cooking spray. Add onion and cook slowly over low-medium heat until tender, about 5 minutes. Add garlic, sugar, eggplant and tomatoes; cook over medium-high heat, stirring occasionally, until eggplant is very soft, about 15 minutes. Cool to room temperature. Stir in vinegar, capers and parsley; season to taste and serve.

Serves 4

Nutrition Facts

Nutrition (per serving): 68.8 calories; 6% calories from fat; 0.6g total fat; 0.0mg cholesterol; 1433.0mg sodium; 422.4mg potassium; 16.3g carbohydrates; 5.1g fiber; 8.3g sugar; 2.1g protein.

French Onion Soup

1 tsp unsalted stick margarine
1 onion, chopped
1 1/2 cups low-sodium beef broth
2 oz French bread, cut into
two slices and toasted
1/3 cup shredded part-skim mozzarella cheese

Preheat the broiler. In a medium saucepan, melt the margarine. Add the onion and cook, stirring as needed, until softened, about 5 minutes. Add the broth; bring to a boil. Reduce the heat and simmer, uncovered, until the onion is very tender, about 3 minutes.

Place one slice of the toast in each of two flameproof soup bowls; pour the soup over the toast. Sprinkle each with the cheese and broil until the cheese is melted and lightly browned, about 1 minute. Serve at once.

Serves 2

Nutrition Facts

Nutrition (per serving): 180.0 calories; 30% calories from fat; 6.0g total fat; 12.0mg cholesterol; 326.0mg sodium; 19.0g carbohydrates; 1.0g fiber; 12.0g protein.

Fresh Corn and Goat Cheese Salad

4 pieces corn on the cob
3 medium scallions, two diced, one chopped
1/4 cup diced sweet red pepper
2/3 oz soft-type goat cheese - (about 2 Tbs)
2 Tbs fresh lemon juice
1/8 tsp table salt, or to taste
1/8 tsp freshly-ground black pepper, or to taste

Steam or microwave corn until tender. Cool, then cut kernels from cob. Stir together corn, diced scallions and red pepper in a medium bowl.

Combine chopped scallion, goat cheese and lemon juice in a blender or food processor; process until smooth. Pour over corn mixture and toss well; season to taste with salt and pepper and toss again.

Serves 4

Nutrition Facts

Nutrition (per serving): 80.4 calories; 16% calories from fat; 1.5g total fat; 2.2mg cholesterol; 243.6mg sodium; 223.8mg potassium; 16.3g carbohydrates; 2.3g fiber; 0.9g sugar; 3.2g protein.

Fresh Cream of Tomato Soup with Basil

1 serving cooking spray
2 medium leeks, white parts only, chopped
8 medium ripe beefsteak tomatoes - (abt 3 lbs), cored, chopped
1 tsp dried thyme
1 piece bay leaf
4 cups vegetable broth
12 oz fat-free evaporated milk
1/4 Tbs chopped fresh basil
1/8 tsp table salt, or to taste
1/8 tsp freshly-ground black pepper, or to taste
1 Tbs fresh thyme, for garnish

Coat a large saucepan with cooking spray and set pan over medium heat. Add leeks and sauté until soft, about 5 minutes. Add tomatoes, thyme and bay leaf; cook until tomatoes break down, about 5 minutes.

Add broth and bring to a simmer; reduce heat to low, cover and simmer 10 minutes. Remove from heat and remove bay leaf.

Working in batches, puree tomato mixture in a blender until smooth (be careful not to splatter hot liquid). Return puree to saucepan and set pan over low heat. (Or puree in saucepan using an immersion blender.) Add milk and simmer 1 minute to heat through. Remove from heat and stir in basil; season to taste with salt and pepper. Garnish with thyme and serve.

Serves 6

Nutrition Facts

Nutrition (per serving): 141.3 calories; 11% calories from fat; 1.8g total fat; 4.2mg cholesterol; 672.3mg sodium; 598.6mg potassium; 24.1g carbohydrates; 2.2g fiber; 14.0g sugar; 8.1g protein.

Fresh Curried Corn Soup

2 tsp olive oil
1 cup chopped onion
2 tsp curry powder
4 cups fat-free chicken broth
4 pieces corn on the cob, kernels removed
1/2 lb uncooked red potatoes - (abt 2 large), peeled, chopped
1 1/2 Tbs fresh lemon juice
1 tsp table salt
1/4 cup chopped cilantro or scallion
1/4 cup plain fat-free yogurt
1/4 cup diced tomato

Heat oil in a large saucepan. Add onion; cover and cook over medium heat, stirring occasionally, until softened, about 5 minutes. Add curry powder and cook 30 seconds until fragrant.

Add broth, corn, potatoes, lemon juice and salt to saucepan; bring to a boil over medium-high heat. Reduce heat to medium-low and simmer, partially covered, until potatoes are tender, about 20 minutes; remove from heat.

In a blender, food processor or with an immersion (handheld) blender, puree mixture (in batches if necessary), until smooth. Strain through a fine mesh sieve, pressing on solids to extract as much liquid as possible, into a bowl. Serve hot, or cover and refrigerate up to 2 days.

To serve, stir cilantro or scallions into soup. Spoon into bowls and top with about 2 teaspoons each of yogurt and tomato. Garnish with additional chopped cilantro or scallions, if desired.

Serves 6

Nutrition Facts

Nutrition (per serving): 157.2 calories; 14% calories from fat; 2.7g total fat; 0.6mg cholesterol; 994.7mg sodium; 585.9mg potassium; 32.5g carbohydrates; 4.0g fiber; 4.9g sugar; 5.0g protein.

Garden Salad with Creamy Herb Dressing

1 cup jicama, peeled and julienned
1 cup watercress, chopped
3 cups torn red leaf lettuce
1/2 cup sliced radishes
2 Tbs lime juice
1/4 cup tarragon vinegar
1 Tbs honey
1/2 cup soft tofu
1 tsp olive oil
1 tsp low-sodium soy or tamari sauce
1 Tbs stone-ground mustard
2 tsp minced parsley
1/2 tsp chopped fresh thyme
1/2 tsp minced fresh basil

In a large salad bowl, toss together jicama, watercress, lettuce, and radishes.

In a blender puree lime juice, vinegar, honey, tofu, oil, and soy sauce until creamy. Stir in mustard, parsley, thyme, and basil, and pour over salad. Toss well and serve.

Serves 4

Nutrition Facts

Nutrition (per serving): 77.6 calories; 30% calories from fat; 2.8g total fat; 0.0mg cholesterol; 61.8mg sodium; 300.0mg potassium; 11.6g carbohydrates; 2.8g fiber; 5.6g sugar; 3.6g protein.

Harvest Chicken Chowder

2 tsp olive oil
4 onions, chopped
3 garlic cloves, minced
1 lb boneless skinless chicken breasts, cubed
2 cups low-sodium chicken broth
2 celery stalks, sliced
1 carrot, sliced
1 can pumpkin puree - (15 oz)
1 can evaporated skim milk - (12 oz)
1/4 cup minced parsley
1 Tbs minced fresh sage
= (or 1/2 tspn dried sage)
1 tsp dried thyme leaves
Freshly-ground black pepper, (optional)

In a large nonstick saucepan or Dutch oven, heat the oil. Add the onions and garlic; cook, stirring as needed, until softened, about 5 minutes.

Add the chicken, broth, celery and carrot; bring to a boil. Reduce the heat and simmer, stirring as needed, until the chicken is cooked through and the vegetables are tender, about 10 minutes.

Add the pumpkin, milk, parsley, sage and thyme; return to a boil, stirring as needed. Serve, sprinkled with the pepper (if using).

Serves 4

Nutrition Facts

Nutrition (per serving): 317.0 calories; 16% calories from fat; 6.0g total fat; 65.0mg cholesterol; 269.0mg sodium; 33.0g carbohydrates; 5.0g fiber; 36.0g protein.

Hearty Chicken Vegetable Soup

1 can no-salt-added diced tomatoes - (14 1/2 oz)
3 packets low-sodium instant chicken broth and
seasoning mix
2 carrots, sliced
2 onions, coarsely chopped
2 celery stalks, sliced
1 medium zucchini, diced
3/4 cup elbow macaroni
2 garlic cloves, minced
1/2 lb boneless skinless chicken breast, cut into 1" pieces
1/4 cup minced parsley
1/2 tsp salt
1/4 tsp freshly-ground black pepper

In a large nonstick saucepan or Dutch oven, bring the tomatoes, broth mix and 6 cups water to a boil. Add the carrots, onions, celery, zucchini, macaroni and garlic; return to a boil, stirring as needed. Reduce the heat and simmer, covered, stirring as needed, until the vegetables and macaroni are tender, about 30 minutes.

Increase the heat and stir in the chicken, parsley, salt and pepper; return to a boil. Reduce the heat and simmer, covered, until the chicken is cooked through, about 10 minutes.

Serves 8

Nutrition Facts

Nutrition (per serving): 109.0 calories; 8% calories from fat; 1.0g total fat; 16.0mg cholesterol; 182.0mg sodium; 16.0g carbohydrates; 2.0g fiber; 9.0g protein.

Herbed Split Pea Soup

1 lb green split peas, picked over,
rinsed and drained
4 cups low-sodium vegetable broth
2 leeks - (to 3), cleaned, sliced
2 carrots, diced
1/2 tsp dried marjoram
1/4 tsp freshly-ground black pepper
1/4 tsp grated nutmeg
1/2 package frozen chopped spinach - (10-oz pkg),
thawed
1 Tbs lemon juice

In a large nonstick saucepan or Dutch oven, bring the peas, broth, leeks, carrots, marjoram, pepper, nutmeg and 4 cups water to a boil. Reduce the heat and simmer, covered, until the peas are tender, about 40 minutes.

With a slotted spoon, transfer the vegetables to a blender or food processor. Puree, then return to the saucepan. Stir in the spinach and lemon juice. Cook until heated through, about 5 minutes.

Serves 8

Nutrition Facts

Nutrition (per serving): 2501.0 calories; 74.0mg sodium; 47.0g carbohydrates; 5.0g fiber; 16.0g protein.

Home Made French Dressing

1 cup nonfat yogurt
1 cup ketchup
1/2 cup vinegar
2 Tbs sugar
1/2 tsp prepared mustard

Blend ingredients together. May also add pepper, garlic powder, chopped onion or chopped parsley for a different taste without changing caloric value.

This recipe yields 2 1/2 cups (twenty 2-tablespoon servings).

Serves 20

Nutrition Facts

Nutrition (per serving): 15.0 calories; 50.0mg sodium; 3.0g carbohydrates; 1.0g protein.

Jicama Salad

4 oranges, peeled, sectioned
1 orange, juiced
2 cups jicama, peeled, julienned
1 cucumber, peeled, sliced thin
2 cups cantaloupe, peeled, cubed
1/2 cup red onion, sliced thin rounds
1/4 cup chopped cilantro or parsley
2 Tbs fresh mint
1/2 tsp hot chili powder
1/4 cup lime juice

Peel and section oranges over a bowl to collect juices. Juice the remaining orange. Place orange sections, jicama, cucumber, melon, onion, cilantro (or parsley) and mint into a large bowl.

Combine the orange juice, lime juice and chili powder. Pour over the jicama mixture. Toss gently, cover and chill. Serve on a lettuce leaf.

Serves 6

Nutrition Facts

Nutrition (per serving): 115.0 calories; 10.0mg sodium; 25.0g carbohydrates; 8.0g fiber; 3.0g protein.

Lettuce Soup

2 tsp unsalted stick margarine
2 celery stalks, chopped
4 scallions, thinly sliced
6 cups shredded green leaf lettuce
4 cups low-sodium vegetable broth
1/4 cup minced parsley
1/4 tsp freshly-ground black pepper
2 Tbs grated Parmesan cheese

In a large nonstick saucepan or Dutch oven, melt the margarine. Add the celery and scallions; cook, stirring as needed, until softened, about 5 minutes.

Stir in the lettuce, broth, parsley, pepper and 1 cup water; bring to a boil. Reduce the heat and simmer, stirring as needed, until the lettuce is wilted, about 5 minutes. Serve, sprinkled with the cheese.

Serves 4

Nutrition Facts

Nutrition (per serving): 83.0 calories; 32% calories from fat; 3.0g total fat; 2.0mg cholesterol; 141.0mg sodium; 11.0g carbohydrates; 1.0g fiber; 3.0g protein.

Manhattan Fish Chowder

1 Tbs olive oil
2 celery stalks, diced
2 onions, chopped
2 garlic cloves, minced
2 cans no-salt-added whole tomatoes - (28 oz ea), coarsely chopped
1/2 cup dry white wine
1 tsp dried basil
1 tsp dried oregano
1/2 tsp dried thyme leaves
1/2 tsp freshly-ground black pepper
1/4 tsp salt
2 lbs sole of flounder fillets, cut into 1" pieces
1/2 cup minced parsley

In a large nonstick saucepan or Dutch oven, heat the oil. Add the celery, onions and garlic; cook, stirring as needed, until softened, about 5 minutes.

Add the tomatoes, wine, basil, oregano, thyme, pepper and salt; bring to a boil. Reduce the heat and simmer, covered, until the flavors are blended, about 25 minutes.

Add the fish and parsley; increase the heat and bring to a boil, stirring gently. Reduce the heat and simmer, uncovered, stirring as needed, until the fish is opaque, about 5 minutes.

Serves 6

Nutrition Facts

Nutrition (per serving): 240.0 calories; 19% calories from fat; 5.0g total fat; 73.0mg cholesterol; 260.0mg sodium; 15.0g carbohydrates; 3.0g fiber; 32.0g protein.

Mediterranean Bean Salad

10 oz mixed baby greens
15 1/2 oz canned cannellini beans, rinsed, drained
10 medium cherry tomatoes, halved
1/2 cup diced red onion
1/2 tsp olive oil
1 Tbs Dijon mustard
2 Tbs balsamic vinegar
2 Tbs fresh tarragon, minced
2 medium garlic cloves, minced
1/4 tsp table salt
1/8 tsp freshly-ground black pepper

In a large bowl, combine greens, beans, tomatoes and onion.
In a separate bowl, whisk together remaining ingredients for dressing.
Pour over salad and toss well before serving.

Serves 4

Nutrition Facts

Nutrition (per serving): 402.0 calories; 4% calories from fat; 1.9g total fat; 0.0mg cholesterol; 221.2mg sodium; 2203.8mg potassium; 72.4g carbohydrates; 18.6g fiber; 0.0g sugar; 27.2g protein.

Pumpkin Soup

1 large onion, minced
2 cups defatted chicken stock or vegetable broth
1 1/2 cups pureed cooked pumpkin
1/2 tsp dried oregano
1/4 tsp hot-pepper sauce
1/4 cup toasted pumpkin seeds

In a 2-quart saucepan, cook the onions in 2 tablespoons of the stock or broth until limp.

Add the remaining stock, pumpkin, oregano and hot-pepper sauce. Simmer for 15 minutes.

Serve sprinkled with pumpkin seeds.

Serves 4

Nutrition Facts

Nutrition (per serving): 60.0 calories; 19% calories from fat; 1.3g total fat; 1.0mg cholesterol; 16.0mg sodium; 4.3g fiber.

Saffron Carrot Soup

2 cups low-sodium vegetable broth
3 carrots, cut into 2" chunks
4 onions, chopped
3 small all-purpose potatoes, peeled, and
cut into 2" chunks
1 cup parsley leaves
1 tsp olive oil
2 carrots, sliced
1 cup sliced mushrooms
1/2 tsp freshly-ground black pepper
1/8 tsp saffron threads, crumbled
1/2 cup plain nonfat yogurt
Minced parsley, for garnish

In a large nonstick saucepan or Dutch oven, bring the broth, carrot chunks, onions, potatoes, parsley leaves and 7 cups water to a boil. Reduce the heat and simmer, covered, until the vegetables are tender, about 1 hour.

Meanwhile, in a large nonstick skillet, heat the oil. Add the sliced carrots and mushrooms; cook, covered, stirring as needed, until the carrots are tender, about 10 minutes, adding 1 tablespoon water at a time, if necessary. Stir in the pepper and saffron.

With a slotted spoon, transfer the vegetables from the saucepan to a blender or food processor. Puree, then return them to the broth. Whisk in the yogurt and stir in the sautéed vegetables; cook, stirring as needed, until heated through, 2 to 3 minutes. Serve, garnished with the minced parsley.

Serves 6

Nutrition Facts

Nutrition (per serving): 143.0 calories; 6% calories from fat; 1.0g total fat; 78.0mg sodium; 30.0g carbohydrates; 5.0g fiber; 5.0g protein.

Southwestern Egg Salad

6 whole hard-boiled eggs
2 medium scallions, finely chopped
1 tsp canned green chili peppers, drained, chopped
1 Tbs minced fresh cilantro
1/2 small sweet red pepper, finely chopped
1/4 cup fat-free mayonnaise
1 Tbs salsa
1/4 tsp ground cumin
1/4 tsp table salt
1/8 tsp freshly-ground black pepper

Peel eggs; mash with a fork in a large bowl. Add remaining ingredients and mix thoroughly to coat. (Note: If desired, trim fat and cholesterol by using 2 whole eggs and 8 egg whites instead of 6 whole eggs.)

Serve egg salad in a cored bell pepper, over mixed greens or on its own in a bowl.

Serves 4

Nutrition Facts

Nutrition (per serving): 151.1 calories; 57% calories from fat; 9.6g total fat; 363.2mg cholesterol; 405.6mg sodium; 163.8mg potassium; 4.6g carbohydrates; 0.7g fiber; 3.2g sugar; 11.0g protein.

Tomato, Avocado and Golden Beet Salad

3/4 lb golden variety beets - (abt 4 med), scrubbed, and the tops removed
4 medium tomatoes, cut 1/4" wedges = (different colors or heirloom if possible)
1 medium ripe Haas avocado, cut 1/2" cubes
1 small red onion, cut in half, and sliced into thin half moons
4 tsp extra-virgin olive oil
4 tsp red wine vinegar
1/4 tsp table salt
1/4 tsp freshly-ground black pepper
1 Tbs chopped fresh basil
1 Tbs chopped fresh chives

Place a medium saucepan filled with water over high heat. Add beets, bring back to a boil and reduce heat to medium; simmer until beets pierce easily with the point of a sharp knife, about 25 minutes.

Remove beets from pan and place under cold running water until cool enough to handle. Peel beets with a vegetable peeler and cut into 1/2-inch wedges; place beets in a large bowl.

Add tomato, avocado, onion, oil, vinegar, salt and pepper to bowl; toss to combine. Top mixture with basil and chives and serve.

Serves 4

Nutrition Facts

Nutrition (per serving): 281.7 calories; 22% calories from fat; 7.6g total fat; 0.0mg cholesterol; 506.0mg sodium; 1847.4mg potassium; 50.3g carbohydrates; 16.6g fiber; 32.4g sugar; 8.8g protein.

Tomato-Tofu Bisque

1 Tbs unsalted stick margarine
1 onion, chopped
1 Tbs all-purpose flour
2 cans no-salt-added diced tomatoes -, (14 1/2 oz ea)
2 cups low-sodium vegetable broth
1 tsp dried oregano
1/4 tsp freshly-ground black pepper
3/4 lb reduced-fat soft tofu (reserve 1/2 cup of the liquid)
1/2 cup minced parsley
2 Tbs minced dill
1 Tbs honey

In a large nonstick saucepan or Dutch oven, melt the margarine. Add the onion and cook, stirring as needed, until softened, about 5 minutes. Add the flour and cook, stirring constantly, until the flour is lightly browned, about 1 minute.

Add the tomatoes, broth, oregano and pepper; bring to a boil. Reduce the heat and simmer, covered, until heated through, about 10 minutes.

Meanwhile, in a blender or food processor, puree the tofu and the reserved liquid. Add the tofu, parsley, dill and honey to the tomato mixture; cook, stirring as needed, until just heated through, about 3 minutes.

Serves 4

Nutrition Facts

Nutrition (per serving): 165.0 calories; 31% calories from fat; 6.0g total fat; 72.0mg sodium; 23.0g carbohydrates; 2.0g fiber; 7.0g protein.

Tortellini Soup

1 Tbs unsalted stick margarine
2 cups sliced mushrooms
1 garlic clove, minced
2 cups low-sodium vegetable broth
1 can no-salt-added Italian-style
stewed tomatoes - (14 1/2 oz)
3 cups frozen cheese tortellini
1 package frozen chopped spinach - (10 oz),
thawed, and
squeezed dry
Freshly-ground black pepper, to taste

In a large nonstick saucepan or Dutch oven, melt the margarine. Add the mushrooms and garlic; cook, stirring as needed, until softened, 2 to 3 minutes.

Add the broth, tomatoes and 3 cups water; bring to a boil. Add the tortellini; return to a boil. Reduce the heat and simmer, stirring as needed, until the tortellini is cooked, about 10 minutes. Stir in the spinach and return to a boil. Serve, sprinkled with the pepper.

Serves 6

Nutrition Facts

Nutrition (per serving): 237.0 calories; 22% calories from fat; 6.0g total fat; 23.0mg cholesterol; 265.0mg sodium; 37.0g carbohydrates; 4.0g fiber; 10.0g protein.

Tropical Avocado and Fruit Salad with Creamy Lime Dressing

1 papaya, seeded, peeled, and cubed
2 cups fresh pineapple chunks
1 can water-packed mandarin oranges - (11 oz), drained
1 avocado, seeded, peeled, and diced
1 Tbs snipped fresh mint, (optional)
=== CREAMY LIME DRESSING ===
1/2 cup fat-free plain yogurt
2 Tbs honey
5 tsp fresh lime juice

In a large bowl, combine the papaya, pineapple, oranges and avocados. Add the dressing and gently fold in until the fruit mixture is coated. If desired, sprinkle with the mint to garnish.

Serves 8

Nutrition Facts

Nutrition (per serving): 115.0 calories; 31% calories from fat; 4.0g total fat; 0.0mg cholesterol; 19.0mg sodium; 2.1g fiber.

Zesty Tomato Salad

4 medium tomatoes, chopped 1/2" pieces = (or 2 pints
smaller tomatoes)
1 medium cucumber, seeded, and chopped into 1/2" pieces =
(or use a seedless cucumber)
1/2 medium red onion, chopped 1/2" pieces
1 Tbs lemon zest
1/2 tsp table salt
1/4 tsp freshly-ground black pepper

Toss tomatoes, cucumber, onion, zest, salt and pepper together in a
large bowl; allow to stand for at least 20 minutes.

Serves 6

Nutrition Facts

Nutrition (per serving): 11.7 calories; 9% calories from fat; 0.1g total
fat; 0.0mg cholesterol; 196.0mg sodium; 115.2mg potassium; 2.4g
carbohydrates; 0.8g fiber; 1.2g sugar; 0.5g protein.

Index

E